Mothers Against Drunk Driving

The mission of Mothers Against Drunk Driving is to stop drunk driving and to support the victims of this violent crime.

We're Still MADD

Mothers Against Drunk Driving was started in 1980 after a California woman's daughter was killed by a hit-and-run driver. Incredibly, the driver had been released from jail on bail just two days earlier — for another drunk driving hit-and-run crime.

Determined to stop the tragic loss of life caused by drinking and driving, the girl's mother and others in her community formed the first chapter of MADD.

Today, that one small group of committed women has grown to a nationwide grass-roots movement with 400 chapters across America.

And MADD is not just for mothers. Our more than 3,000,000 members and supporters include fathers, brothers, uncles, and sons. In fact, anyone can join MADD. The only requirement is a commitment to end alcohol- and other drug-impaired driving.

Since MADD was started, 1,400 anti-drunk driving laws have been passed. These laws are helping police, prosecutors, and judges remove impaired drivers from our highways — and keep them off.

But laws alone can't stop people from drinking and driving.

MADD is educating the public about the dangers of impaired driving. Through programs like the Designated Driver and Project Red Ribbon, we're spreading this important message across America — drinking and driving must stop.

After more than a decade of battling drinking and driving, we're still MADD. And we're still committed to ending the senseless injuries and deaths caused by drunk driving.

You Can Help MADD
MADD needs your help — because drinking and driving affects everyone.

Along with the human toll in destroyed lives, drunk driving costs the United States $46 billion every year in direct costs.

As a team, MADD and you are working to keep drunk drivers off our highways. Here are a few ways you can make a difference:

- Make a personal promise to never drink and drive.

- Don't let friends or relatives drive under the influence of alcohol or other drugs.

- Speak out in your community against alcohol- and other drug-impaired driving.

- Support tougher legislation against drunk driving. Tell your local, county, state, and federal representatives that their help is needed to end drinking and driving.

- Use a Designated Driver if you drink when you're out. Encourage friends and relatives to use and to be Designated Drivers.

- Warn the young people in your life about the dangers of underage drinking and impaired driving. Don't let someone else teach them the wrong lessons about drinking and driving.

- Never serve alcohol to anyone under 21 years old or anyone who has had too much to drink.

- Report drunk drivers to the police.

- Remember that a person's ability to drive can be greatly affected by alcohol long before he or she appears to be intoxicated.

Your Help Makes a Difference
Thanks to the help of millions of concerned and committed people across America, alcohol-related traffic deaths have decreased approximately 35 percent since MADD was founded in 1980.

Behind that amazing statistic is a more important fact. The anti-drunk driving movement in this country has saved an estimated

58,000 lives — lives that would have been tragically cut short by alcohol- and other drug-impaired crashes.

But there's so much more hard work ahead of us.

Two out of every five Americans will be involved in an alcohol- or other drug-related crash during their lives. We want to reduce those odds — and protect you from the threat of drinking and driving.

In 1992, an estimated 18,000 people died as the result of alcohol-related crashes on the nation's highways.

Each of those deaths is a solemn reminder that MADD must continue the battle against drinking and driving. And we will continue to do everything possible to make our roads safer — for everyone.

MADD's Goals

Even though alcohol-related traffic fatalities have dropped more than 35 percent since MADD was founded in 1980, the proportion of traffic fatalities that were alcohol-related remains about 46 percent. MADD's goal for the 1990s is to reduce this proportion 20 percent by the year 2000. The "20 By 2000" plan includes:

• *Youth Issues*
Education, prevention, and penalties for alcohol and other drug use by those under age 21, whether driving or not.

• *Enforcement*
Sobriety checkpoints, a blood alcohol content limit of .08, and mandatory testing of drivers involved in fatal and serious injury crashes.

• *Sanctions*
Administrative license revocation, plate or vehicle confiscation for repeat offenders, and equal penalties for death and serious injury DUI/DWI offenses.

• *Self-Sufficiency*
DUI/DWI fines, fees and other assessments to fund programs to prevent, detect, and deter impaired driving.

• *Responsible Marketing & Service of Alcohol*
Uniform closing hours for drinking establishments, Designated Driver programs, server training, and an end to happy hours.

MADD's "Victims" plan to support victims of impaired driving includes:
• *Amendments for Victims Rights*
State constitutional amendments to ensure that victims will be informed of, present at, and heard in the criminal justice process.

• *Compensation for Victims*
Assurance that drunk driving victims have the same eligibility requirements for state crime victim compensation funds as other crime victims.

• *Dram Shop Recovery*
Legislation or case law to allow victims the right to seek financial recovery from servers who have provided alcohol to those who are intoxicated or to minors who then cause fatal or serious injury crashes.

• *Endangerment of Children*
Legislation to enhance the sanctions of convicted impaired drivers who drove with a minor child in the vehicle.

MADD is on Your Side
Mothers Against Drunk Driving is more committed than ever to protecting you, your family, and your friends from the threat of alcohol- and other drug-related driving crashes.

But we want you to know that MADD is only a phone call away if you or anyone you know is ever the victim of a drunk driving crash.

Victims and their families may call our hot line at 800 - GET - MADD. Our trained staff is prepared to give victims immediate emotional support and advice on the criminal justice system. And we'll direct victims to the MADD chapter nearest them, so that they can receive personalized support and understanding for however long they may need it.

MADD can stop the alcohol- and other drug-related crashes that destroy so many lives each year. Please, help us in whatever way you can to make our highways safer. Thank you.

Mothers Against Drunk Driving

If you would like more information on MADD in your local community or how to get more involved, contact:
MADD National Office
511 E. John Carpenter Freeway, Suite 700
Irving, TX 75062
214-744-MADD

For victim assistance, call:
1-800-GET-MADD

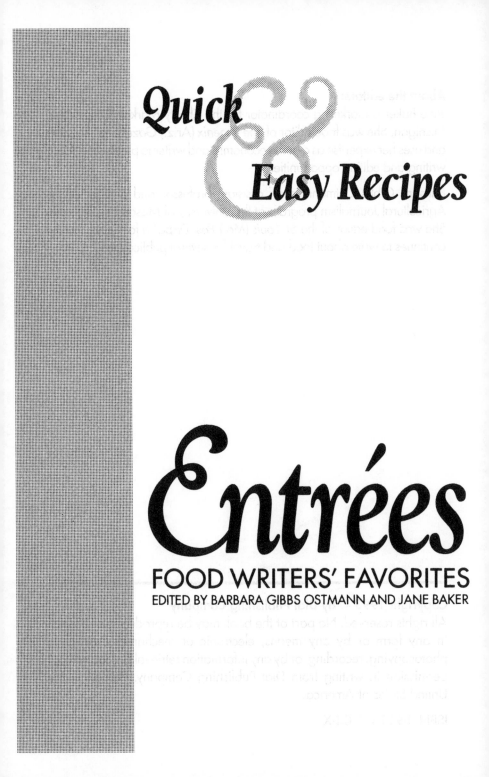

Quick & Easy Recipes

Entrées

FOOD WRITERS' FAVORITES
EDITED BY BARBARA GIBBS OSTMANN AND JANE BAKER

About the editors:
Jane Baker is marketing coordinator for the Cherry Marketing Institute in Michigan. She was food editor of *The Phoenix* (Ariz.) *Gazette* for 14 years and uses her expertise as a home economist and writer to pursue free-lance writing and editing opportunities.

Barbara Gibbs Ostmann is an assistant professor and director of the Agricultural Journalism program at the University of Missouri - Columbia. She was food editor of the *St. Louis* (Mo.) *Post-Dispatch* for 16 years and continues to write about food and travel for several publications.

ISBN 0-911479-04-X

Contents

1 Information About MADD

10 Contributing Writers

12 Introduction

13 Tips for Quick & Easy Meals

17 Meatless

37 Fish & Seafood

61 Poultry

89 Pork

109 Beef

135 Lamb, Game & Other Meats

Contributing Writers

Barbara Mihalevich Arciero, Free-Lance Food Writer, Sacramento, CA
Jane Baker, Free-Lance Writer, East Lansing, MI
Laura Barton, Free-Lance Writer, Portland, OR
Louise Bentley, *Chippewa Herald Telegram*, Chippewa Falls, WI
Barbara Burklo, (Retired) *Santa Cruz Sentinel*, Santa Cruz, CA
Toni Burks, *Roanoke Times & World-News*, Roanoke, VA
Narcisse S. Cadgène, Free-Lance Writer, New York, NY
Sally Cappon, *Santa Barbara News-Press*, Santa Barbara, CA
Leona Carlson, (Retired) *Rockford Register Star*, Rockford, IL
Debra Carr-Elsing, *The Capital Times*, Madison, WI
Arlette Camp Copeland, *The Macon Telegraph*, Macon, GA
Dorothy Cunningham, Free-Lance Writer, Morenci, MI
Louise Dodd, *Courier Herald*, Dublin, GA
Beth Whitley Duke, *Amarillo Globe-News*, Amarillo, TX
Clara H. Eschmann, *The Macon Telegraph*, Macon, GA
Barbara Fisher, *This Week Publications*, Farmingdale, NY
Diana Fishlock, *The Express-Times*, Easton, PA
Carolyn Flournoy, *The Times*, Shreveport, LA
Paula M. Galusha, Free-Lance Home Economist, Tulsa, OK
Janet Geissler, *Lansing State Journal*, Lansing, MI
Jane Gray, *Ludington Daily News*, Ludington, MI
Patricia G. Gray, *The Express-Times*, Easton, PA
Teri M. Grimes, *The Bradenton Herald*, Bradenton, FL
Lorrie Guttman, *Tallahassee Democrat,* Tallahassee, FL
Suzanne Hall, *The Chattanooga Times*, Chattanooga, TN
Delia A. Hammock, *Good Housekeeping*, New York, NY
Alice Handkins, Free-Lance Food Writer, Wichita, KS
Zack Hanle, *Bon Appétit* magazine, New York, NY
Monetta L. Harr, *Jackson Citizen Patriot*, Jackson, MI
Constance Hay, Free-Lance Food Writer, Columbia, MD
Jim Hillibish, *The Repository*, Canton, OH
Mary Beth Jung, Free-Lance Food Writer, Grafton, WI

Susan Manlin Katzman, Free-Lance Food Writer, St. Louis, MO
Sue Kurth, *Beloit Daily News*, Beloit, WI
Stacy Lam, *The Macon Telegraph*, Macon, GA
Florence Larson, *Norfolk Daily News*, Norfolk, NE
Lori Longbotham, Free-Lance Food Writer, Astoria, NY
Beth W. Orenstein, *The Express Times*, Easton, PA
Barbara Gibbs Ostmann, Food Writer, St. Louis, MO
Christine Randall, *The Post and Courier*, Charleston, SC
Doris Reynolds, *Naples Daily News*, Naples, FL
Marion Riedl, *Ludington Daily News*, Ludington, MI
Sally Scherer, *The Macon Telegraph*, Macon, GA
Mary D. Scourtes, *The Tampa Tribune*, Tampa, FL
Kathleen Stang, Food Writer, Seattle, WA
Caroline Stuart, Free-Lance Writer, Greenwich, CT
Jeanne Voltz, Cookbook Author, Pittsboro, NC
Ann Corell Wells, *The Grand Rapids Press*, Grand Rapids, MI
Kasey Wilson, *The Vancouver Courier*, Vancouver, BC, Canada
Barbara Yost, *The Phoenix Gazette*, Phoenix, AZ

Introduction

Everyone is in a hurry today. And nowhere is the effect more evident than in the kitchen. Grandma used to spend hours preparing family meals, often baking bread and fixing homemade desserts. Today, hardly anyone has that kind of time, not even Grandma.

However, a lack of time doesn't mean giving up taste-tempting, homemade food. Food writers love good food — but like other people, they, too, are caught in the time bind.

Here, then, is a special collection of their favorite main course recipes. All of them can be prepared quickly and easily, generally with commonly available ingredients. *Quick & Easy Recipes: Entrées* combines not only tried-and-true personal favorites but also regional specialties. It's a collection of recipes that are good not only for family meals but also for entertaining guests.

On the following pages are some tips and hints for speeding up meal preparation. In addition, each of the recipes in the book includes a brief introduction that tells you something about the recipe and may even offer an extra time-saving tip or an idea for a quick accompaniment.

We would like to make it clear that these recipes are the contributors' favorites. The publisher makes no claim that the recipes are original. When possible, credit has been given where credit is due. In many cases, however, the recipes just evolved or have been handed down through families or exchanged by friends and neighbors, and it is difficult, if not impossible, to say from where they came.

We hope you find this book to be a unique collection of quick and easy recipes that will delight your family as well as your guests.

Happy cooking!

— Jane Baker and Barbara Gibbs Ostmann
Editors of *Food Writers' Favorites*
Quick & Easy Recipes: Entrées

Tips for Quick & Easy Meals

How do some people put an entire meal on the table in 30 minutes? Organization is the key. Here are some basic time-savers that cooks in a hurry find useful.

The Basics

Probably the best principle to follow is to be realistic when planning your time. Use variations of favorite recipes when time is short, saving new or innovative recipes for days when you are not so rushed. It will save you time and increase your chances for success if you use kitchen-tested recipes. All of the recipes in this book have been tested by experienced food writers and editors.

Here are some other suggestions:

- Consider saving time versus saving money. For example, buying shredded cheese can save preparation time, but it costs more. If you have the time, purchase cheese in bulk, shred a quantity and store it in plastic bags or containers in the freezer. The cheese is ready to use when you need it. The same technique works with a number of other food items.
- Think in terms of how you can save time when preparing a recipe. Do the cucumbers really need peeling? If possible, clean and chill items ahead of time.
- Plan leftovers so Sunday's dinner can be reheated quickly for a weekday meal.
- If time allows, prepare two casseroles at once. Freeze one for later use. The same applies to soups, stews and many other recipes.

Kitchen Organization

Time spent getting your kitchen in working order will end up being time saved when you are preparing recipes.

- Keep utensils close to where they are used and make sure you have enough of them to avoid washing them after each step in a recipe.
- Keep baking pans together in one cupboard, if possible. Arrange pots and pans near the stove.
- Keep a supply of hot pads and trivets within easy reach of the stove and microwave oven, so you don't waste time hunting for them when needed.
- Keep knives sharp and in a handy location. Sharp knives make cutting chores go faster.
- Organize your pantry or cupboards so staple items are easy to find. It's important to have spices and herbs where they are visible. Some cooks store spices and herbs in alphabetical order; others use spice rack organizers.
- Stock up on shelf-stable ingredients, such as pasta, beans and rice. Make sure you keep plenty of sugar and flour on hand as well as various condiments. Canned broths, tomatoes, oils and vinegars are always needed. Having these

items on hand saves time shopping for ingredients and provides the basics for many spur-of-the-moment recipes.

- Organize the refrigerator and freezer, keeping often-used items within easy reach. Milk, eggs and butter or margarine are a few of the basics to have on hand in the refrigerator.

Grocery Shopping

Be creative in getting this chore done easily and quickly. One idea is to enlist the help of children or your spouse. Give them specific items to get and bring back to the shopping cart. With practice, they will be-come aware of the exact items you often purchase.

Here are some other ideas:

- Plan meals, so you can shop for a week's worth of groceries at one time.
- A grocery list is a must if you are interested in saving time. Take the time at home to make an accurate list of what you need, then follow the list closely in the store. As a general rule, buy only those items on the list. This saves money as well as time.
- Shopping when stores are less crowded is a good time saver.
- When picking up only a few items, shop at a store you know. That way you won't waste time searching for items.

Preparation

Quick and easy recipe preparation actually begins the moment that you arrive home with the groceries. For example, divide meat into serving portions. Wrap individual chops and steaks so that they can be frozen separately for faster thawing. Also, shaping ground meat in a doughnut shape will allow it to thaw faster.

When you are preparing a recipe, try these ideas:

- Read through the recipe before you begin, to make sure you know how to prepare it and that you have all the ingredients.
- For minimum preparation time, assemble all the ingredients and utensils you need before you begin.
- Peel, chop, slice and mince all items at one time.
- Open all cans at once.
- Do steps ahead of time when possible.
- Keep the kitchen clean and uncluttered as you work. It's a good idea to keep a sink of hot soapy water ready to wash dishes and utensils as you work.
- Don't overlook the help that may be available to you. Children, a spouse or live-in grandparents can help clean fruits and vegetables, wash or dry mixing bowls and utensils and set the table. Training someone to be useful in the kitchen generally pays off later.

Cooking

By selecting recipes carefully, you can avoid recipes that take a long time to cook or involve several time-consuming steps.

- Broiling and stove-top cooking are usually faster than oven cooking. However, it is often possible to cook more than one item at the same time in the oven.

- While you have something in the oven or simmering on the stove, work on another recipe.

- Sometimes it is possible to shorten cooking time by cutting ingredients into smaller pieces.

- Serve your food buffet- or family-style. Serving and arranging individual plates is time consuming.

Microwave Tips

Of all the appliances in your kitchen, a microwave oven has the greatest poten-tial for helping to prepare quick and easy meals. Some of the recipes in this book give microwave instructions. In other recipes, where a conventional cookery method is suggested, you might prefer melting butter or doing other steps in the microwave.

Here are some suggestions for using the microwave oven efficiently:

- Cooking times vary greatly, depending on the wattage of the oven. Use cooking times listed as a guide, but always check the food one to two minutes before the cooking time has elapsed.

- Use the microwave to reheat foods quickly. If possible, reheat only the portions needed.

- Smaller portions reheat more quickly than larger ones.

- A microwave oven can quickly thaw ingredients needed for a recipe.

- Cut food into pieces of approximately the same size, so they cook in the same amount of time.

- Round dishes heat food more evenly than square ones.

- Glass dishes are good for microwave cooking, because you can see what's happening with the food. Glass measuring cups are great for sauces and soups. Plastic storage containers can be used for heating food in a micro-wave, but it is best to use those specifically designated "microwave safe." Others might warp or melt.

- The food closest to the outside edge of a dish cooks fastest. If you have uneven pieces of meat or vegetables, place the thickest ends at the edge of the plate.

- If you have foods that are small and all the same size, arrange them in a circle around the edge of the dish so they cook in the same amount of time.

Meatless 🍄 🍄 🍄 🍄 🍄

18 Baked Deviled Eggs

19 Black Bean Salad Española

20 Brie Strata with Fruit Salsa

21 Glorified Steamed Veggies with Rice

22 Greek Spaghetti

23 Green Spaghetti

24 Lentil-Vegetable Casserole

25 Macaroni and Cheese Supreme

26 Mediterranean Stir-Fry

27 Mushroom Casserole

28 Mushroom Lover's Tart

29 Pasta Primavera Pronto

30 Pasta Provençale

31 Scrambled Egg Bake

31 Spanish Tofu

32 Spicy Rice and Beans

33 Stuffed Zucchini

34 Sweet-Sour Tofu Stir-Fry

35 Vegetarian Taco Salad

36 Zucchini Pie

Baked Deviled Eggs

Suzanne Hall
Food Editor, *The Chattanooga Times*, Chattanooga, TN

Deviled eggs are traditional picnic fare, but in this recipe, shared by a Chattanooga cooking teacher, they get a classy touch for use on the brunch or supper table. The eggs are good served over rice, toasted English muffins or waffles. For a fancier dish, serve them in puff pastry shells. However you serve them, they're quick, easy and tasty.

Makes 6 to 8 servings

6 hard-cooked eggs
1 cup plus 3 tablespoons dairy
   sour cream, divided
2 teaspoons prepared mustard
1/4 teaspoon salt
2 tablespoons butter or margarine
1/3 cup chopped onion

1/2 cup chopped green bell
   pepper
1 can (10 3/4 ounces) condensed
   cream of mushroom soup,
   undiluted
1/4 cup chopped pimento
1/2 cup grated Cheddar cheese

Peel eggs; cut in half, lengthwise. Remove yolks; reserve whites. Mash yolks; blend in 3 tablespoons sour cream, mustard and salt. Fill reserved whites with yolk mixture.

Heat butter in a medium saucepan. Add onion and bell pepper; sauté until tender. Remove from heat. Stir in mushroom soup, pimento and remaining 1 cup sour cream; mix well.

Pour half of the soup mixture into a shallow 1 1/2-quart baking dish. Arrange filled eggs, cut-side up, in a single layer over soup mixture. Pour remaining soup mixture over eggs. Top with cheese. Bake in a preheated 350-degree oven 20 minutes, or until heated through. Let stand 5 minutes before serving. Serve over hot cooked rice, toasted English muffin halves, waffles or puff pastry shells.

Please don't drink and drive.

Black Bean Salad Española

Mary D. Scourtes
Food Writer, *The Tampa Tribune*, Tampa, FL

Black beans are a staple in Tampa, where the Spanish use this nutritious legume in soups, dips and sauces. The '90s method is to turn them into salads. You can take a short-cut by using the canned beans available in most supermarkets; rinse the beans with water and drain thoroughly to remove excess salt.

Makes 8 servings

1 teaspoon olive oil
1 clove garlic, minced
1/2 cup salsa or picante sauce
   (store-bought or homemade)
2 tablespoons lemon juice
1 teaspoon ground cumin
Pinch salt
4 cups torn Romaine lettuce leaves
1 can (15 ounces) black beans,
   rinsed and well drained

1 medium red bell pepper,
   julienned
1 medium tomato, cut up
2 green onions, julienned
   (green and white parts)
4 hard-cooked eggs, peeled and
   quartered

Heat oil in a skillet; add garlic and sauté briefly. Add salsa, lemon juice, cumin and salt; mix well. Cook over medium heat 2 to 3 minutes.

In a large salad bowl, combine Romaine leaves, black beans, bell pepper, tomato and green onions.

Pour hot dressing over Romaine mixture; toss. Top with hard-cooked eggs.

Brie Strata with Fruit Salsa

Mary Beth Jung
Free-Lance Food Writer, Grafton, WI

Here's a new twist to "comfort food," a strata made with creamy Brie. This do-ahead recipe is perfect for the busy hostess because it can be prepared the night before. I like to serve this to large or small gatherings; simply double or triple the recipe as needed. Garnish with Fruit Salsa for a colorful and flavorful touch.

Makes 6 servings

Butter	4 eggs
8 to 10 slices white bread, crusts removed	1 1/2 cups milk
	1 teaspoon salt
1 pound Brie cheese, rind removed, cut into cubes	Paprika
	Fruit Salsa (see recipe)

Butter one side of each slice of bread. Place half the bread slices, buttered-side up, in a greased 9x9x2-inch baking pan. Top with half the Brie cubes. Repeat with remaining bread and Brie.

Beat eggs in a medium mixing bowl with a wire whisk or fork. Add milk and salt to eggs; mix well. Pour egg mixture over bread and Brie in baking pan. Sprinkle paprika on top.

Let stand at least 30 minutes before baking, or refrigerate overnight. (If strata has been refrigerated, let stand at room temperature 30 minutes before baking.)

Bake in a preheated 350-degree oven 35 to 40 minutes. To serve, cut strata into squares and top with Fruit Salsa.

Fruit Salsa

Makes 2 cups salsa

1 pint fresh strawberries, stemmed, diced	1 tablespoon honey
1 Anjou pear, diced	1 tablespoon fresh lime juice

In a mixing bowl, combine strawberries, pear, honey and lime juice; mix well. Serve at room temperature over Brie Strata.

"Impaired" means a person's ability to drive safely is diminished by alcohol.

Glorified Steamed Veggies with Rice

Alice Handkins
Free-Lance Food Writer, Wichita, KS

Prepare steaming plates of rice and vegetables for your family when you want a quick-to-prepare, one-dish meal. It's bright, colorful, full of low-calorie wholesome nutrition, and absolutely delicious. This recipe was developed by my sister, Linda Alldritt, for her family. She is frequently asked for the recipe by people lucky enough to sample it at her house.

Makes 4 servings

Water	1 small zucchini, sliced
1/2 teaspoon salt	1 cup grated Cheddar cheese
3/4 cup uncooked long-grain rice	1 cup alfalfa sprouts
1 1/4 cups sliced carrots	1 large tomato, diced
1 1/4 cups cauliflower pieces	3 green onions, thinly sliced
1 1/4 cups broccoli florets	Soy sauce

In a 2 1/2-quart saucepan, bring 1 1/2 cups water and salt to a boil; add rice. Cover with a tight-fitting lid. Bring mixture to a boil, then remove pan from heat. Let stand 30 minutes. Do not lift the lid during this time.

Bring 2 cups water to a boil in a steamer or saucepan. Add carrots; steam, covered, 2 minutes, or until carrots just begin to get tender. Add cauliflower and broccoli; steam, covered, 2 to 3 minutes, or until the cauliflower and broccoli just begin to get tender. Add zucchini; steam, covered, 2 to 3 minutes, or until all vegetables are tender-crisp. (The steamer or saucepan must be kept tightly covered during the steaming process.) Thoroughly drain vegetables.

Divide cooked rice among 4 dinner plates. Spoon steamed vegetables over the rice. Top each serving with cheese, alfalfa sprouts, tomatoes and green onions. Pass soy sauce at the table.

Greek Spaghetti

Mary D. Scourtes
Food Writer, *The Tampa Tribune*, Tampa, FL

When I've had an extra-tough day at work, forgotten to thaw anything for dinner and come home ravenous, it's time to turn to speedy spaghetti. In most cases, the crowd at my house chants for Greek Spaghetti, a dish that goes from pantry to table in minutes.

Makes 4 to 6 servings

1 pound uncooked spaghetti, linguine or fettuccine	1 teaspoon dried oregano
2 tablespoons (or less) olive oil	Juice of 1 lemon
1 medium onion, chopped	1/3 cup grated Romano or Parmesan cheese or combination
2 cloves garlic, minced	
1 jar (6 ounces) marinated artichoke hearts	4 ounces feta cheese, crumbled
12 Greek or Italian-style black olives	

Cook pasta according to package directions. Drain and set aside.

Heat oil in a large skillet. Add onion and garlic; sauté 1 to 2 minutes.

Drain artichokes, reserving liquid; cut artichoke hearts in half and set aside. Add reserved artichoke liquid, olives, oregano and lemon juice to onion-garlic mixture; mix well. Heat 2 to 3 minutes. Add reserved artichoke hearts; heat through.

Combine cooked pasta, artichoke mixture, Romano cheese and feta cheese. Serve immediately.

A person's ability to drive is impaired at blood alcohol content levels as low as .02.

Green Spaghetti

Paula M. Galusha
Free-Lance Home Economist, Tulsa, OK

When our 16-year-old son was just a little fellow, he was always asking me to make one of his favorite dishes, which he called Green Spaghetti. Those of us in the culinary world know it as Fettuccine with Pesto Sauce. Because the only cooking required for this recipe is boiling the pasta, this makes a quick dinner. Serve it with a fresh garden salad and some hot French bread and the meal is complete. If you grow basil in your garden, make the pesto in the summer when basil leaves are plentiful and freeze it for future use. Fresh basil leaves can be purchased in some supermarkets, as can frozen pesto.

Makes 4 servings

1 1/2 cups loosely packed fresh
    basil leaves, rinsed and
    well drained
1/2 cup grated Parmesan cheese
1/3 cup olive oil

2 tablespoons walnut pieces
1/2 teaspoon salt
1 large clove garlic
8 ounces uncooked fettuccine or
    other pasta

In container of electric blender, combine basil leaves, cheese, olive oil, walnuts, salt and garlic. Blend on medium speed until smooth. Do not overblend, or mixture will separate. If sauce is too thick, add 1 tablespoon hot water; blend.

Cook fettuccine or other pasta according to package directions; drain. Toss pesto sauce with hot fettuccine and serve immediately.

Lentil-Vegetable Casserole

Barbara Burklo
Food Editor (Retired), *Santa Cruz Sentinel*, Santa Cruz, CA

Our daughter Kathy Burton uses little meat in preparing meals for her family. She gave me this vegetarian casserole recipe several years ago, and I've found that both our vegetarian and non-vegetarian friends think it is delicious. The lentils and cheese provide protein, the varied herbs and other ingredients provide lots of flavor, and best of all, it can be prepared quickly, even though the ingredient list is rather long.

Makes 6 servings

1 package (12 ounces) lentils, rinsed and drained
2 cups water
1 can (16 ounces) tomatoes, undrained, coarsely chopped
2 large onions, chopped
3 cloves garlic, minced
1 bay leaf
1 teaspoon salt
1/4 teaspoon black pepper
1/8 teaspoon dried marjoram
1/8 teaspoon dried sage
1/8 teaspoon dried thyme
2 carrots, thinly sliced
1/2 cup thinly sliced celery
1 small green bell pepper, chopped
2 tablespoons chopped fresh parsley
2 cups grated Cheddar or Monterey Jack cheese

In a 13x9x2-inch baking dish, combine lentils, water, tomatoes with their liquid, onions, garlic, bay leaf, salt, pepper, marjoram, sage and thyme. Cover tightly with aluminum foil. Bake in a preheated 375-degree oven 30 minutes.

Stir in carrots and celery. Return to oven and bake, covered, 40 minutes, or until lentils and vegetables are tender.

Stir in bell pepper and parsley. Sprinkle cheese over top. Return to oven and bake, uncovered, 5 minutes, or until cheese melts.

Wait at least one hour per drink consumed before you drive.

Macaroni and Cheese Supreme

Barbara Fisher
Food Writer, *This Week Publications*, Farmingdale, NY

As a child, I always looked forward to the nights my mom served macaroni and cheese for dinner. At the time, it was truly one of my favorite dishes. During the early years of my marriage, my mother-in-law introduced me to her version of this dish, to which she added mozzarella cheese and tomatoes. With a penchant for macaroni and cheese and a desire to create a hearty, flavorful dish for my family, I combined the recipes of my mother and mother-in-law, made a few modifications and formulated a recipe that's sure to satisfy any appetite. It can be prepared ahead of time, refrigerated and heated when needed.

Makes 6 servings

8 ounces uncooked
  elbow macaroni
1/4 cup butter or margarine
1/4 cup all-purpose flour
2 1/2 cups milk
2 1/2 cups grated Cheddar
  cheese, divided

1 teaspoon Worcestershire sauce
Salt and white pepper, to taste
1 can (16 ounces) tomatoes,
  drained
1 cup shredded
  mozzarella cheese

Cook macaroni according to package directions; drain and set aside.

Melt butter in a saucepan over medium heat; blend in flour and stir to a smooth consistency. Slowly stir in milk. Cook, stirring constantly, until sauce thickens (do not boil). Remove from heat. Add 2 cups Cheddar cheese; stir to blend. Add Worcestershire sauce. Season cheese sauce to taste with salt and white pepper.

Place cooked macaroni in a 2-quart baking dish; add cheese sauce and mix thoroughly. Cut tomatoes into small pieces; spread across top of macaroni mixture. Sprinkle remaining 1/2 cup Cheddar cheese and the mozzarella cheese over tomatoes. Bake in a preheated 350-degree oven 35 minutes, or until hot and bubbly.

Mediterranean Stir-Fry

Dorothy Cunningham
Free-Lance Writer, Morenci, MI

A trip to the Mediterranean is high on my list of "things to do" — someday. In the meantime, I satisfy my yearnings with this zesty Italian dish found in a local church cookbook. I revised it to update the cooking method. Serve this stir-fry with Italian sausage, fresh fruit and a loaf of crusty bread.

Makes 4 to 6 servings

3 tablespoons olive oil
1 large onion, sliced
  1/2-inch thick
1 medium eggplant, unpeeled,
  cut into 1/2-inch cubes
3 to 4 tablespoons water
1/2 teaspoon dried basil
1/2 teaspoon dried oregano
1/8 teaspoon black pepper

1/2 pound fresh mushrooms,
  sliced
1 red bell pepper, cut into
  1-inch squares
1 green bell pepper, cut into
  1-inch squares
1 large tomato, cut into wedges
Grated Parmesan cheese

Heat oil in a wok or large skillet. Add onion and eggplant. Toss and stir over high heat about 5 minutes, or until vegetables are tender. Reduce heat to medium-high; stir in water, basil, oregano, pepper, mushrooms and red and green bell peppers. Cover and let steam 5 minutes. Arrange tomato wedges on top. Cover and cook 2 minutes. Sprinkle with Parmesan cheese just before serving.

Drunk driving is a crime in virtually every state and the District of Columbia.

Mushroom Casserole

Barbara Yost
Feature Writer, *The Phoenix Gazette*, Phoenix, AZ

I've been making this full-bodied casserole for almost 20 years, and it never fails to please a party crowd. No matter what else I serve, this casserole receives the most attention and I always get requests for the recipe. My little secret is that I've never tasted it! I don't like mushrooms and I don't eat mushrooms, so I judge the success of this recipe by its appearance and the rave reviews. I'm told that it's out of this world. That many friends can't be wrong!

Makes 6 servings

1 1/2 pounds fresh mushrooms
6 tablespoons butter or margarine, divided
1 1/2 cups chopped onions
1/2 cup chopped celery
1/2 cup chopped green bell pepper
1/2 cup mayonnaise

6 to 8 slices white bread
2 eggs, beaten
1 1/2 cups milk
1 can (10 3/4 ounces) condensed cream of mushroom soup, undiluted
1 cup grated Romano cheese

Rinse mushrooms and pat dry with paper towels; chop mushrooms. Melt 4 tablespoons butter in large skillet. Add mushrooms, onions, celery and bell pepper; sauté until just tender. Remove from heat. Stir in mayonnaise; mix well.

Use remaining 2 tablespoons butter to spread on both sides of bread slices; cut bread into cubes. Spread about half of the bread cubes in a lightly greased 13x9x2-inch baking dish. Spoon mushroom mixture evenly over bread. Cover with remaining bread cubes.

In a medium bowl, combine eggs and milk; mix well. Pour over mixture in baking dish. Cover and refrigerate overnight.

Before baking, pour mushroom soup over mixture in baking dish. Sprinkle cheese on top. Bake in a preheated 350-degree oven 1 hour, or until hot and bubbly.

Mushroom Lover's Tart

Laura Barton
Free-Lance Writer, Portland, OR

Mushrooms are a favorite ingredient, and I use them enthusiastically in salads, soups, sauces and entrées. In this recipe, they star in a rich and satisfying meatless entrée. I usually serve this tart with a tossed green salad. Sometimes I make miniature mushroom tartlets to serve as hors d'oeuvres.

Makes 4 main-course servings

1 (9-inch) pie crust, unbaked
2 tablespoons butter or margarine
1 pound fresh mushrooms, sliced
1 cup chopped fresh parsley
4 green onions, finely chopped

1 cup dairy sour cream
1 tablespoon Worcestershire sauce
3 eggs, slightly beaten
1/2 teaspoon black pepper

Bake pie crust in a preheated 350-degree oven 5 to 10 minutes, or until partly baked. Let cool.

Heat butter in a large skillet. Add mushrooms; sauté over medium heat until lightly browned. Add parsley and green onions; cook, stirring, until limp. Remove from heat.

In a small bowl, combine sour cream, Worcestershire sauce, eggs and pepper; mix well. Stir sour cream mixture into mushroom mixture; mix well. Spoon mixture evenly into partly baked pie crust.

Bake in a preheated 400-degree oven 25 minutes, or until a knife inserted in the middle comes out clean.

Note: You can use a combination of shiitake, chanterelle and/or button mushrooms, if desired.

Ask what police, judges and lawmakers are doing to end drunk driving.

Pasta Primavera Pronto

Zack Hanle
Editor-at-Large, *Bon Appétit* magazine, New York, NY

A grandson studying engineering at Lehigh University is a good amateur cook with a passion for pasta in all forms. He cooks his own meals at school and asked me to develop a recipe for him that would take little time to prepare, yet provide a variety of nutrients. This recipe is the result.

Makes 4 servings

6 quarts water
1 tablespoon salt
1 package (8 ounces)
　uncooked spaghetti
1/4 cup olive oil

3 large cloves garlic, minced
1 package (10 ounces) frozen
　mixed vegetables, thawed
1 cup grated Romano cheese

Bring water and salt to boiling in a large pot. Add spaghetti; boil 8 to 10 minutes, or until spaghetti is al dente (firm but tender).

While pasta is cooking, heat olive oil in a large skillet; add garlic and sauté until browned. Add thawed vegetables to garlic; stir-fry over medium heat until vegetables are hot, but still firm and crisp.

Drain spaghetti; divide among four plates. Top each portion of pasta with one-fourth of the vegetable mixture. Serve at once. Pass the cheese for those who desire it.

Note: Leftover pasta and vegetables can be mixed, refrigerated, then reheated.

Pasta Provençale

Suzanne Hall
Food Editor, *The Chattanooga Times*, Chattanooga, TN

Neville Forsythe is the chef/owner of a restaurant in Chattanooga. His Jamaican background and love of French cooking make his menu versatile and appealing. This colorful, quick dish is a regular item on his lunch menu. It makes a good evening entrée as well. Use whatever pasta you have on hand.

Makes 6 to 8 servings

About 1 tablespoon vegetable oil
3 yellow onions, sliced
3 green bell peppers, sliced
1 clove garlic, crushed
3 zucchini, diced into
  medium pieces
3 yellow summer squash, diced
  into medium pieces

4 tomatoes, diced into
  large pieces
1 teaspoon dried basil, or to taste
Salt and black pepper, to taste
1 cup heavy cream
12 ounces uncooked pasta of
  your choice

Heat oil in large skillet. Add onions, bell peppers and garlic; sauté 2 minutes. Add zucchini and yellow squash; sauté 1 minute. Add tomatoes and basil. Season to taste with salt and pepper. Drain excess juices. Add cream; cook over low heat, stirring gently, until thickened. Correct seasoning, if needed.

Meanwhile, cook pasta in rapidly boiling water 7 to 10 minutes. (Follow package directions for al dente.) Drain.

Place hot pasta on serving platter or individual plates. Spoon vegetable mixture on top.

Vote for tougher drunk driving laws.

Scrambled Egg Bake

Barbara Yost
Feature Writer, *The Phoenix Gazette*, Phoenix, AZ

This is a lovely and easy entrée for breakfast or brunch. Cut it into squares and serve it with an assortment of pastries and fruit.

Makes 4 servings

6 eggs
1/3 cup milk
1/4 pound mild or sharp Cheddar cheese, cut into small cubes
Salt and black pepper, to taste

In a large mixing bowl with a wire whisk or fork, beat eggs until frothy. Stir in milk; mix well. Add cheese. Season with salt and pepper. Pour into a buttered 2-quart baking dish. Bake in a preheated 350-degree oven 30 minutes. Serve immediately.

Spanish Tofu

Diana Fishlock
Feature Writer, *The Express-Times*, Easton, PA

This is a wonderfully versatile recipe. I've made it using only onion or pepper, with different cheeses, or with tomato paste. I've added fresh garlic, cumin or parsley. I've served it over pasta or couscous. I've let it simmer a long time or briefly. It always tastes great!

Makes 2 servings

6 ounces tofu (use fresh tofu,
    if available), cut into
    bite-size cubes
1 can (8 ounces) tomato sauce
3/4 cup canned tomatoes
    (plain or Italian-style), drained
1 green bell pepper, diced

1 small onion, diced
1/2 teaspoon dried oregano
1/2 teaspoon dried basil
1/8 teaspoon garlic powder
Shredded mozzarella cheese
Hot cooked rice

In a large non-stick skillet, combine tofu, tomato sauce, tomatoes, bell pepper, onion, oregano, basil and garlic powder; mix well. Cook over medium heat, stirring occasionally, 10 minutes, or until mixture is hot. Sprinkle cheese on top. Serve tofu-vegetable mixture over rice.

Send "thank you" letters to legislators who sponsor stronger drunk driving laws.

Spicy Rice and Beans

Alice Handkins
Free-Lance Food Writer, Wichita, KS

A combination of beans and rice provides a healthful and economical alternative to a meat dish. Because this recipe calls for lots of green peppers, onions and tomatoes, there is no need to serve a vegetable side dish. For a quick meal, stir up a batch of corn bread, toss a green salad and serve them with this easy main course.

Makes 4 servings

1 1/2 cups water
1/2 teaspoon salt
1 cup uncooked long-grain rice
1 can (16 ounces) tomatoes, undrained, coarsely chopped
2 tablespoons butter or margarine
1/2 cup finely chopped green bell pepper

1/2 cup finely chopped onion
1 can (16 ounces) ranch-style beans, undrained
2 tablespoons chili powder (or to taste)
1 teaspoon hot pepper sauce (or to taste)

Bring water to a boil in a 2 1/2-quart saucepan. Add salt, rice and tomatoes with their liquid. Cover with a tight-fitting lid. Simmer over low heat about 25 minutes, or until rice is done.

Melt butter in a small skillet. Add bell pepper and onion; sauté over medium heat until vegetables are tender-crisp.

Add sautéed vegetables, beans with their liquid, chili powder and hot pepper sauce to rice mixture; stir to mix. Add up to 1/2 cup water if mixture seems too thick. Simmer 10 to 15 minutes to blend flavors. Serve hot.

Send a "letter to the editor" expressing your support for stronger drunk driving legislation.

Stuffed Zucchini

Alice Handkins
Free-Lance Food Writer, Wichita, KS

Zucchini gardeners are always on the lookout for new and different recipes — as well as friends to give zucchini to. This year I was fortunate to have been given some zucchini, along with an interesting recipe for stuffed zucchini. I modified the recipe and ended up with a wonderful vegetarian main dish, but you could cut the zucchini into small portions and use it as a vegetable side dish.

Makes 4 main-course servings

1 large zucchini (about 10 inches long and 3 inches wide)
3 tablespoons butter or margarine
1/4 cup chopped onions
1 clove garlic, finely minced
1 cup sliced fresh mushrooms
3/4 cup ricotta cheese
1/2 cup shredded mozzarella cheese

2 tablespoons grated Parmesan cheese
1/2 cup soft white bread crumbs
1 teaspoon dried Italian herbs
1/2 teaspoon salt
1/8 teaspoon black pepper

Cut zucchini in half lengthwise and crosswise. Scoop out the interior pulp, leaving a 1/4-inch-thick shell; set the 4 shells aside. Dice the zucchini pulp.

Melt butter in a large skillet. Add onions and garlic; sauté 2 minutes. Add diced zucchini pulp; sauté 2 minutes. Add mushrooms; sauté just until mushrooms are tender.

In a mixing bowl, combine ricotta, mozzarella and Parmesan cheeses, bread crumbs, Italian herbs, salt and pepper; mix well. Stir cheese mixture into sautéed vegetables; mix well.

Place reserved zucchini shells in a 13x9x2-inch glass baking pan. Fill each zucchini shell with vegetable-cheese mixture. Bake, uncovered, in a preheated 350-degree oven 25 to 30 minutes, or until zucchini shells are tender and vegetable-cheese mixture is lightly browned.

Sweet-Sour Tofu Stir-Fry

Laura Barton
Free-Lance Writer, Portland, OR

Stir-frys are a favorite way to prepare fresh and flavorful meals quickly on busy days. Tofu especially fits into my "fast and easy" repertoire. When I prepare this stir-fry, my only disappointment is that there are seldom any leftovers to enjoy later.

Makes 6 servings

2 tablespoons cornstarch
1/2 cup cider vinegar
1/4 cup firmly packed
    brown sugar
2 tablespoons soy sauce
1/4 teaspoon dry mustard
1 can (16 ounces) crushed
    pineapple in juice, undrained
1 tablespoon vegetable oil
2 cloves garlic, minced
1 teaspoon minced fresh ginger
    (or 1/2 teaspoon
    ground ginger)

1 onion, chopped
1 green bell pepper, sliced
1 red bell pepper, chopped
1 zucchini, sliced
2 cups sliced fresh mushrooms
1 cup peeled, sliced jicama
    (or one 8-ounce can sliced
    water chestnuts, drained)
2 cups fresh snow peas
1 pound firm tofu, drained and
    cut into cubes
Hot cooked rice

In a small saucepan, stir together cornstarch and vinegar. Add brown sugar, soy sauce, dry mustard and pineapple with its juice. Simmer over medium heat until thickened. Set sweet-and-sour sauce aside.

Heat oil in a wok or large skillet. Add garlic, ginger and onion; stir-fry 1 minute. Add green and red bell peppers, zucchini, mushrooms, jicama and snow peas; stir-fry 2 to 4 minutes. Stir in tofu and reserved sauce. Heat through. Serve over rice.

Note: Frozen tofu can be used; let it thaw and drain, then cut it into strips or cubes.

Support Sobriety Checkpoints. They deter drunk drivers and save lives.

Vegetarian Taco Salad

Alice Handkins
Free-Lance Food Writer, Wichita, KS

Everyone has a special version of Taco Salad. This is my favorite combination of ingredients. It only takes five to 10 minutes to prepare the ingredients for this nutritious main-dish salad. The recipe easily can be halved or doubled, depending on the number of servings needed. Ingredient amounts can be adjusted for individual preferences. I like lots of crisp nacho cheese tortilla chips sprinkled on top of the salad, rather than mixed into the salad.

Makes 2 large or 4 medium servings

1/2 cucumber, peeled and diced into 1/4-inch pieces
1 avocado, peeled and cubed
3 ounces Colby cheese, cut in 1/4-inch cubes
2/3 cup chopped celery
1 tomato, diced
1/2 cup sliced black olives
1/2 cup chopped green bell pepper

4 green onions, thinly sliced
1 can (16 ounces) ranch-style beans, undrained
4 cups shredded iceberg lettuce
2/3 cup store-bought Catalina-style salad dressing
1 1/2 cups crushed nacho cheese tortilla chips

In a large salad or mixing bowl, combine cucumber, avocado, cheese, celery, tomato, olives, bell pepper, green onions and beans with their liquid; mix well. Add lettuce and toss to combine.

Drizzle salad dressing over salad; toss well. (Use more or less salad dressing, according to personal preference.) Divide the salad among serving plates. Pass crushed tortilla chips at the table.

Zucchini Pie

Jane Baker
Free-Lance Writer, East Lansing, MI

I once made the mistake of telling friends who are avid gardeners that I liked zucchini. Naturally, I spent the summer trying to use up the bounty from their gardens. Some of the recipes I used that summer are long forgotten, but I prepare this one often, even in winter when I have to buy zucchini at the supermarket. It makes a fast weekday meal, but I also like to make it for Sunday supper because the leftovers are easy to reheat for lunch or even dinner during the week.

Makes 4 to 6 servings

2 medium zucchini, cubed
1 medium onion, chopped
1 medium tomato, chopped
2 cloves garlic, minced
1 cup grated Cheddar cheese
1 1/2 cups milk

3/4 cup buttermilk baking mix
3 eggs, slightly beaten
1/2 teaspoon coarsely ground black pepper
1/4 teaspoon dried thyme
Dash hot pepper sauce

In a lightly greased 9-inch deep-dish pie plate, combine zucchini, onion, tomato and garlic. Sprinkle cheese over vegetables.

In a medium mixing bowl, combine milk, baking mix, eggs, pepper, thyme and hot pepper sauce; mix well. Pour evenly over vegetable-cheese mixture.

Bake in a preheated 375-degree oven 35 to 40 minutes, or until golden brown. Let cool 5 minutes before cutting into wedges.

Please say "crash" — not "accident" — when talking about alcohol-related collisions.

Fish & Seafood

38 Baked Fish Fillets

39 Baked Fish Supreme

40 Baked Shrimp with Feta Cheese

41 Barbecued Fish Fillets

42 Dieter's Stir-Fry

43 Easy Baked Fish in Sauce

44 Grilled Mussels with Curry Butter

45 Italian-Style Broiled Fish

46 Laotian Seafood Stir-Fry

47 New Orleans-Style Barbecued Shrimp

48 Pacific Rim Salmon

49 Scallops Acadia

50 Scallops Alfredo

51 Shrimp Casserole

52 Shrimp Jambalaya

53 Shrimp Stroganoff

54 Spaghetti with Clam Sauce

55 Stuffed Orange Roughy

56 Sun Scallops

57 Tuna Casserole Deluxe

58 Tuna Medallions with Sesame Seeds

59 Tuna Steaks Provençale

60 Tuna Steaks with Tomatillo Salsa

Baked Fish Fillets

Barbara Burklo
Food Editor (Retired), *Santa Cruz Sentinel*, Santa Cruz, CA

I adapted this fish recipe from one given to me by Marge Buck of Santa Cruz. For a speedy dinner, put the fish in the oven to bake, then cook potatoes in the microwave oven, and stir-fry a combination of thinly sliced zucchini and carrots seasoned with a touch of dill weed. The whole meal is ready in 20 to 25 minutes.

Makes 2 to 3 servings

1 pound boneless fish fillets
   (snapper or any other
   firm fish)
2 tablespoons mayonnaise
2 tablespoons dairy sour cream

2 tablespoons finely chopped
   green onions
2 tablespoons grated
   Parmesan cheese

Place well-drained fish fillets in a shallow, oven-proof dish or pan. In a small bowl, combine mayonnaise, sour cream, green onions and Parmesan cheese. Pour mayonnaise mixture over fish. Bake, uncovered, in a preheated 400-degree oven 10 to 15 minutes, or until fish flakes easily and is browned on top. Serve immediately.

Note: Reduced-calorie or light mayonnaise and sour cream can be substituted, if desired.

Drunk driving is no accident.

Baked Fish Supreme

Carolyn Flournoy
Food Columnist, *The Times*, Shreveport, LA

Lakes, ponds, rivers and bayous abound in Louisiana, so fresh-water fishing is an ongoing sport. Several of our friends share their largesse with us, which makes for an easy and economical meal. One friend who cooks fish two or three nights a week gave me her special recipe, which I use for family and parties. It's so easy — and the best! I serve the fish with rice, noodles or new potatoes.

Makes 6 to 8 servings

2 tablespoons margarine or butter
1 large onion, finely chopped
3/4 cup evaporated milk
1 tablespoon Worcestershire sauce
Juice of 1 lemon
3 pounds fresh-water fish fillets
   (bass, perch, etc.)

Salt and black pepper, to taste
1 tablespoon chopped
   fresh parsley
1 tablespoon paprika

Heat margarine in a large skillet. Add onion; sauté until slightly brown. Add evaporated milk, Worcestershire sauce and lemon juice; stir to mix.

Pat fish fillets dry with paper towels. Rub fillets with salt and pepper. Place fish in a large baking dish; pour sauce over fish. Sprinkle parsley and paprika over sauce.

Bake, uncovered, in a preheated 375-degree oven 25 to 30 minutes, basting frequently.

Note: Ocean fish fillets can be prepared the same way.

Baked Shrimp with Feta Cheese

Ann Corell Wells
Food Editor, *The Grand Rapids Press*, Grand Rapids, MI

Shrimp, because it has become more reasonably priced, is a favorite "fast food" at my house. I keep frozen shrimp in the freezer and thaw them quickly in the microwave oven before peeling them. This recipe is a combination of several, using flavors my family likes. Don't omit the feta cheese; it really makes this dish.

Makes 4 servings

1 1/2 pounds raw shrimp, unpeeled
1/4 cup olive oil
1 clove garlic, minced
1 can (28 ounces) plum tomatoes, drained
1 green onion, sliced (green and white parts)
1/2 teaspoon dried basil

1/2 teaspoon dried oregano
Dash cayenne pepper
Salt, to taste
Lemon-pepper seasoning salt, to taste
1/2 cup (or more, to taste) crumbled feta cheese
Juice of 1 lemon
Minced fresh parsley

Shell and devein shrimp. Heat oil in a large skillet. Add shrimp and garlic; sauté about 30 seconds, or just until shrimp turn pink. Remove shrimp; cut large shrimp in half; set aside.

Add tomatoes to same skillet, breaking them up with a wooden spoon. Stir in green onion, basil, oregano and cayenne. Season with salt and lemon-pepper seasoning salt. Cook over low heat 10 minutes, stirring occasionally.

Divide reserved shrimp among 4 ramekins or scallop shells (or put them all in one pie plate or other baking dish). Spoon equal amounts of sauce over shrimp; sprinkle feta cheese on top.

Bake in a preheated 350-degree oven about 10 minutes, or until bubbly. Squeeze lemon juice over top; garnish with parsley. Serve immediately.

Alcohol-impaired driving is no joke.

Barbecued Fish Fillets

Janet Geissler
Food Editor, *Lansing State Journal*, Lansing, MI

Barbecued chicken, barbecued pork, barbecued beef. For a change of pace — and a time-saving one, at that — why not try barbecued fish fillets? The barbecue sauce in the recipe is simple and uses ingredients you probably have on hand. If you're really pressed for time, you can substitute your favorite prepared barbecue sauce for the homemade one in this recipe.

Makes 4 to 6 servings

5 tablespoons butter or margarine, divided
1/2 cup chopped onions
1 pound frozen fish fillets, thawed, cut into serving-size pieces
Salt and black pepper, to taste
1/2 cup ketchup

1/3 cup lemon juice
1/4 cup water
2 teaspoons granulated sugar
2 teaspoons Worcestershire sauce
2 teaspoons prepared mustard
Chopped fresh parsley

Preheat an electric skillet to 360 degrees. Add 2 tablespoons butter; heat until melted. Add onions; cook until golden. Transfer onions to a plate and reserve.

Add remaining 3 tablespoons butter to skillet; heat until melted. Add fish pieces; cook until lightly brown, turning carefully with a spatula. Spread reserved cooked onions over fish. Season with salt and pepper.

In a small bowl, combine ketchup, lemon juice, water, sugar, Worcestershire sauce and mustard; mix well. Pour barbecue sauce over fish.

Reduce skillet temperature to about 220 degrees. Simmer mixture about 20 minutes, or until fish flakes easily. Serve immediately, garnished with parsley.

Dieter's Stir-Fry

Dorothy Cunningham
Free-Lance Writer, Morenci, MI

Stir-fried fish? With broccoli? That was my initial reaction when a dieting friend gave me this recipe to add to my collection of quick-to-fix, low-calorie main courses. It turned out to be delicious and has since become a favorite at our house, even when we're not dieting.

Makes 4 servings

1 pound fresh or frozen cod or
 flounder fillets
1 small bunch fresh broccoli
2 tablespoons vegetable oil
1 medium onion, sliced into
 1/8-inch-thick rings

1 rib celery, sliced
1 clove garlic, minced
1/2 teaspoon dried oregano
1 teaspoon salt (or to taste)
Dash black pepper
1 tablespoon lemon juice

Cut fish fillets into bite-size pieces. (If using frozen fish, let it thaw slightly.) Cut broccoli stems into 1/4-inch slices; reserve florets.

In a wok or large skillet, heat oil just to smoking point. Add sliced broccoli, onion, celery, garlic and oregano; stir-fry over high heat 5 minutes. Add fish pieces, salt, pepper and lemon juice. Bring to a boil.

Add reserved broccoli florets. Reduce heat and simmer, covered, 5 to 10 minutes, or until fish flakes easily with a fork. Serve immediately.

Tell the young people in your life that the national drinking age is 21.

Easy Baked Fish in Sauce

Lorrie Guttman
Food Editor, *Tallahassee Democrat*, Tallahassee, FL

North Florida is blessed with an abundance of fresh seafood, which around here is usually served fried. But frying is fattening, so I generally bake fish. A friend of mine who's a dedicated weight-watcher shared a recipe in which fish fillets are cooked in a mixture based on orange juice, another Florida favorite. I added some ground ginger, which blends well with the orange flavor.

Makes 2 to 3 servings

3 fish fillets
  (about 1/4 pound each)
1/2 cup orange juice
1 tablespoon lemon juice
1 teaspoon onion powder
1 teaspoon ground ginger

1/4 teaspoon black pepper
1/4 cup chopped green onions
2 tablespoons chopped
  fresh parsley
1 lemon, sliced

Spray baking dish with cooking spray. Arrange fish fillets in baking dish.

In a small bowl, combine orange juice, lemon juice, onion powder, ginger and pepper; mix well. Pour mixture over fish. Sprinkle green onions over fish.

Bake, covered, in a preheated 450-degree oven 20 to 25 minutes, depending on the thickness of the fillets. Transfer fish and sauce to serving dish. Garnish with parsley and lemon slices.

Grilled Mussels with Curry Butter

Teri M. Grimes
Assistant Features Editor, *The Bradenton Herald*, Bradenton, FL

As folks who live in other seafaring states can tell you, a person can get mighty spoiled by the availability of fresh fish any time it's wanted. While we in Florida have long indulged ourselves with snapper, grouper, blue crabs, shrimp, lobster and other treasures from the sea, mussels have not been a part of our daily diets. With the growth of mussel farms (just like the catfish farms of the last decade), this tasty mollusk is reaching a wider audience. I like to prepare them on the grill, seasoned with this rich curry butter that is just right for dunking.

Makes 4 servings

2 pounds mussels
3 tablespoons butter or margarine,
  softened
2 cloves garlic, pressed
1 teaspoon curry powder
1/2 teaspoon ground cumin

1/8 teaspoon salt
1 large lime
1 cup diced red bell pepper
1/4 cup finely chopped
  fresh parsley
French bread

Scrub the mussels and pull out the beards. Refrigerate until ready to use.

In a small bowl, combine butter, garlic, curry powder, cumin and salt; mix well.

Cut lime in half crosswise; cut one half into thin slices and the other half into 4 wedges.

Divide mussels into 4 servings; arrange each portion in a single layer on a large piece of aluminum foil. Dot with curry butter mixture. Sprinkle with bell pepper and parsley. Top with lime slices. Loosely close foil to make four packets.

Place foil packets over medium-hot coals; grill 5 to 10 minutes, or until mussels have opened. Discard any mussels that do not open.

Serve with wedges of lime and lots of French bread to soak up the juices.

The minimum drinking age of 21 saves about 1,000 lives each year.

Italian-Style Broiled Fish

Kathleen Stang
Food Writer, Seattle, WA

This recipe is endlessly adaptable. Choose any variety of firm, mild fish fillets, such as halibut, ling cod, red snapper, Pacific rockfish or cod. Remove any pin bones, then tuck the thin edges of the fillets under to make pieces of even thickness. In summer, vine-ripened tomatoes are, of course, the best. In winter, canned tomatoes make a good alternative.

Makes 4 servings

1 pound firm white fish fillets
Salt and black pepper, to taste
1 large or 2 small tomatoes,
    peeled, seeded and chopped
2 tablespoons minced fresh chives
    or chopped green onion

2 teaspoons chopped fresh basil
    (or 3/4 teaspoon dried)
2 teaspoons olive oil
1/4 cup shredded Monterey Jack
    or Jarlsberg cheese

Cut fish into 4 serving pieces. Season with salt and pepper. Place fish in an oiled shallow broiler-proof baking pan.

In a small bowl, combine tomatoes, chives, basil and olive oil; spoon evenly over fish. Broil 4 to 6 inches from the heat, allowing 10 minutes per inch of thickness of fish, or until fish just begins to flake when tested with a fork.

Sprinkle cheese over fish; broil 30 seconds to 1 minute, or until cheese melts.

Laotian Seafood Stir-Fry

Suzanne Hall
Food Editor, *The Chattanooga Times*, Chattanooga, TN

Each year, international students at the University of Tennessee at Chattanooga sponsor a food festival. This recipe from a young Laotian woman is delicious and easy to prepare. If the cost of seafood is too high, you can substitute boneless chicken breast cut into thin strips.

Makes 8 to 10 servings

1/4 cup peanut oil
2 pounds raw, peeled shrimp or
    crab meat or cooked lobster
    (or a combination), cut into
    bite-size pieces
2 cloves garlic, minced
1 onion, chopped
1/2 cup carrot strips
1 red bell pepper, cut into cubes

1 green bell pepper, cut into cubes
1 cup broccoli florets
1/2 cup fresh or frozen snow peas
1/2 cup cauliflower florets
1/4 cup sliced green onions
    (green and white parts)
2 tablespoons soy sauce
Salt and black pepper, to taste

In a wok or large skillet, heat oil over medium heat. Add raw shrimp or raw crab meat and garlic. Cook, stirring, until shrimp begins to turn pink.

Add onion and carrots. Increase heat to high and cook, stirring constantly, 1 minute. Add cooked lobster (if using), red and green bell peppers, broccoli, snow peas, cauliflower, green onions and soy sauce. Stir-fry 5 minutes, or until vegetables are tender-crisp. Season with salt and pepper. Serve immediately.

Tell youngsters how they can "party" safely without alcohol.

New Orleans-Style Barbecued Shrimp

Susan Manlin Katzman
Free-Lance Food Writer, St. Louis, MO

This shrimp dish comes to St. Louis tables via New Orleans. Although the recipe calls for a little of a lot of ingredients, the only real work is in measuring. Everything is made in, and served from, one skillet, making clean-up a breeze. The cook doesn't even have to peel the shrimp because part of the charm is that diners peel their own, licking the flavorful sauce from their fingers as they eat. Just be sure to serve this dish with crusty French bread and plenty of napkins.

Makes 4 to 6 servings

1 1/2 pounds jumbo
   (21-25 count) raw shrimp,
   unpeeled
6 tablespoons unsalted butter
3 tablespoons olive oil
3 tablespoons chili sauce
1 1/2 tablespoons lemon juice
1 tablespoon Worcestershire sauce
2 cloves garlic, minced

1 teaspoon minced fresh parsley
3/4 teaspoon liquid smoke
1/2 teaspoon dried oregano
1/2 teaspoon paprika
1/2 teaspoon dried thyme
1/4 to 1/2 teaspoon hot
   pepper sauce
Salt, black pepper and cayenne
   pepper, to taste

Rinse shrimp in cold water and pat dry. Set aside.

In a large (about 10-inch) skillet, combine butter, olive oil, chili sauce, lemon juice, Worcestershire sauce, garlic, parsley, liquid smoke, oregano, paprika, thyme and hot pepper sauce. Add salt, pepper and cayenne to taste. Bring mixture to a simmer, stirring constantly; simmer 5 minutes, stirring frequently.

Add shrimp. Turn heat to high and cook, stirring often, 5 to 10 minutes, or until shrimp curl and turn pink. Do not overcook. Serve immediately, with lots of napkins.

Pacific Rim Salmon

Toni Burks
Food Editor, *Roanoke Times & World-News*, Roanoke, VA

It wasn't too many years ago that the only economical way to enjoy salmon was from a can. Today, fresh salmon in all its forms — whole, steaks, fillets — is available and reasonable in price throughout the year. We like it best in the summer, cooked on the grill, and especially as the star for the Fourth of July patio supper. A marinade originally used for chicken is a nice touch for the fish.

Makes 4 servings

4 salmon steaks or fillets
(about 1 1/2 pounds total)
1/2 cup pineapple juice
1/4 cup soy sauce
2 tablespoons coarsely chopped
fresh parsley
2 tablespoons prepared
horseradish

2 teaspoons honey
1/2 teaspoon freshly ground
black pepper
5 green onions, coarsely chopped
(green and white parts)
2 tablespoons sesame oil
4 curly lettuce leaves

Arrange salmon steaks in a shallow baking dish. In a small bowl, combine pineapple juice, soy sauce, parsley, horseradish, honey and pepper; pour over salmon. Sprinkle green onions on top. Cover and refrigerate 1 hour. Turn salmon steaks; cover and return to refrigerator for another hour.

Preheat grill to medium-high, or charcoal briquets to medium-hot. Remove salmon steaks from marinade, reserving marinade. Arrange salmon on oiled grid or in wire fish basket. Add sesame oil to reserved marinade; mix well. Cook salmon 7 minutes, basting frequently with marinade. Turn and cook 5 minutes, basting regularly, until salmon flakes easily when pricked with a fork.

Bring remaining marinade to a boil in a small saucepan on edge of grill; simmer 5 minutes.

To serve, place a ruffled lettuce leaf on each of 4 dinner plates. Top each lettuce leaf with a salmon steak. Drizzle a small portion of the warmed marinade over salmon. Serve immediately.

Help plan an alcohol-free prom or graduation party.

Scallops Acadia

Kathleen Stang
Food Writer, Seattle, WA

We were camping in Maine's Acadia National Park several years ago when an autumn storm blew in. The prediction was for just a brief disturbance, so we left the tent pitched in the campground and headed for a cozy bed-and-breakfast inn. The proprietor suggested a nearby restaurant where local scallops—broiled in this simple honey-lemon marinade—were the specialty of the evening,

---

Makes 4 servings

1/4 cup honey
3 tablespoons lemon juice
1 1/2 tablespoons vegetable oil
1/2 teaspoon grated lemon peel

1/8 teaspoon hot pepper sauce
1 pound raw scallops
Hot cooked rice (optional)

In a medium bowl, combine honey, lemon juice, oil, lemon peel and hot pepper sauce. Pat scallops dry with paper towels; stir into honey marinade. Marinate 15 minutes (while you cook the rice) or up to 1 hour, stirring occasionally.

Arrange scallops and marinade in a single layer in a broiler-proof baking dish. Broil 4 inches from the heat 4 to 7 minutes (depending on size of scallops), or until scallops are opaque and lightly brown. Serve scallop mixture over rice, if desired.

Scallops Alfredo

Doris Reynolds
Food Columnist, *Naples Daily News*, Naples, FL

This is one of the simplest, yet most elegant, pasta dishes I have ever served. Any kind of shellfish can be used. On special occasions I have used lobster meat, but I find that mild sea or bay scallops combine best with the sauce. You could use shrimp or a mixture of shrimp, scallops and lobster — just use your imagination!

Makes 6 to 8 servings

1 pound bay or sea scallops
3 tablespoons olive oil
1 cup sliced fresh mushrooms
3 cloves garlic, finely minced
2 cups half-and-half or
    heavy cream

Salt and black pepper, to taste
1 pound uncooked
    angel hair pasta
Grated Parmesan cheese
    (optional)

If using sea scallops, dice them into quarters. Heat oil in a large, heavy skillet. Add mushrooms and garlic; gently sauté without allowing them to brown. Add scallops; cook, stirring occasionally, about 2 minutes, or until scallops begin to soften. Stir in half-and-half; cook over low heat until liquid reduces by about half. Season with salt and pepper.

Meanwhile, cook pasta according to package directions. Drain.

Pour hot scallop mixture over hot angel hair pasta; toss well. Serve immediately. Pass Parmesan cheese at the table.

Tell your legislators that you endorse a .00 blood alcohol content for youth under 21.

Shrimp Casserole

Christine Randall
Assistant Features Editor, *The Post and Courier*, Charleston, SC

Because I live on the coast, fresh seafood is always available in abundance. Shrimp is one of my favorites. In fact, in this part of the country, you can cast a net into any inlet and catch your own. This particular recipe is good for a dinner party because you can do some of the preparation ahead of time.

Makes 6 to 8 servings

1 1/2 pounds raw shrimp,
   unpeeled
1 tablespoon lemon juice
3 tablespoons vegetable oil
3/4 cup uncooked rice
2 tablespoons butter or margarine
1/4 cup minced green bell pepper
1/4 cup minced onion
1 can (10 3/4 ounces) condensed
   cream of tomato soup,
   undiluted

1 cup heavy cream
1/2 cup slivered almonds, divided
1 teaspoon salt
1/8 teaspoon black pepper
1/8 teaspoon ground mace
Cayenne pepper, to taste
Paprika

Early in the day or the day before: Shell and devein shrimp, then cook shrimp in boiling salted water 5 minutes. Drain. Place shrimp in 2-quart baking dish. Sprinkle lemon juice and oil over shrimp. Refrigerate shrimp mixture.

Cook rice according to package directions. Refrigerate cooked rice.

About 1 hour 10 minutes before serving time: Melt butter in a large skillet. Add bell pepper and onion; sauté. Add onion mixture, chilled cooked rice, tomato soup, cream, 1/4 cup almonds, salt, pepper, mace and cayenne to chilled shrimp mixture in baking dish; mix well. Top with remaining 1/4 cup almonds and paprika. Bake, uncovered, in a preheated 350-degree oven 55 minutes. Serve hot.

Shrimp Jambalaya

Caroline Stuart
Free-Lance Writer, Greenwich, CT

Jack Davis was a prominent dentist in Tuscaloosa, Ala. His first career training was in hotel and restaurant administration, and his reputation as a first-rate cook was well earned. His parties were legendary and "dinner at Dee and Jack's" was a prized invitation. This is his version of the simple and versatile Jambalaya, a hallmark of Creole cookery that combines rice with meat, vegetables and spices.

Makes 6 servings

2 pounds raw shrimp, unpeeled	Freshly ground black pepper,
1/4 cup butter or margarine	to taste
2 medium onions, chopped	1/2 teaspoon dried thyme
1 green bell pepper, chopped	Hot pepper sauce, to taste
2 tomatoes, seeded and chopped	1 cup uncooked rice
1 rib celery, chopped	2 cups chicken broth
2 teaspoons salt	

Shell and devein shrimp; set aside. Melt butter in a large saucepan. Add onions, bell pepper, tomatoes and celery; cook 10 minutes, or until vegetables are soft but not browned. Add reserved shrimp, salt, pepper, thyme and a dash of hot pepper sauce. Cook over medium heat about 5 minutes, or until shrimp turn pink. Add rice and chicken broth. Bring to a boil, stirring once; reduce heat to medium-low. Simmer, covered, 20 minutes, or until rice is cooked. Serve immediately.

Don't let others teach youngsters the wrong lessons about alcohol.

Shrimp Stroganoff

Laura Barton
Free-Lance Writer, Portland, OR

I love to prepare dishes that are not only quick and easy, but also elegant enough to serve when entertaining. Originally this recipe called for lots of sour cream and butter, but I reduced the amount of fat and added some yogurt, and it tastes just as delicious.

Makes 6 servings

4 teaspoons butter or margarine,
   divided
1/4 cup minced onion
1 1/2 pounds peeled,
   cooked shrimp
1/2 pound fresh mushrooms,
   quartered

1 tablespoon all-purpose flour
1 cup plain yogurt
1/2 cup dairy sour cream
1 teaspoon black pepper
1/2 cup canned sliced
   water chestnuts
Hot cooked rice or pasta

Melt 1 teaspoon butter in a large skillet. Add onion; sauté until soft. Add shrimp; sauté 3 to 5 minutes. Transfer shrimp mixture to a dish; keep warm.

In the same skillet, melt remaining 3 teaspoons butter. Add mushrooms; sauté over high heat, stirring constantly, until light brown. Sprinkle flour over mushrooms and mix well; cook 2 minutes.

Reduce heat to low. Stir in reserved shrimp mixture, yogurt, sour cream, pepper and water chestnuts; cook 2 to 3 minutes.

Serve immediately over rice or pasta.

Spaghetti with Clam Sauce

Delia A. Hammock
Nutrition and Fitness Editor, *Good Housekeeping*, New York, NY

> *My definition of a truly quick-and-easy entrée is one that can be made from ingredients always on hand in my cupboard. But, fast and convenient aren't enough. I insist a dish must be healthful, too. My lower-fat version of spaghetti with clam sauce has been a personal favorite for years.*

Makes 2 servings

1 can (10 ounces) whole baby clams	1 tablespoon dried parsley
2 tablespoons olive oil	Pinch crushed red pepper
2 teaspoons minced garlic	Salt and freshly ground black pepper, to taste
1/4 teaspoon dried basil	4 ounces uncooked spaghetti
1/4 teaspoon dried oregano	Grated Parmesan cheese

Drain clams, reserving liquid. Heat oil in a 1-quart saucepan over medium heat. Add garlic; cook until lightly brown. Add basil, oregano, parsley, crushed red pepper and reserved clam liquid; heat to boiling. Reduce heat to low; simmer 10 minutes to blend flavors. Add clams; cook, stirring occasionally, until heated through. Season to taste with salt and pepper.

While clam sauce is simmering, cook spaghetti according to package directions. Drain.

Serve clam sauce over hot spaghetti. Pass Parmesan cheese at the table.

Tell young people about the dangers of underage drinking.

Stuffed Orange Roughy

Monetta L. Harr
Food Editor, *Jackson Citizen Patriot*, Jackson, MI

Since we switched to a low-fat diet, my husband and I are always looking for new ways to prepare fish. My husband, Jerry, found and used a recipe for orange roughy, which called for plain bread crumbs. One day he decided to jazz it up a bit, and used the one-step stuffing mix we had in the cupboard. The herbs in the stuffing were perfect for the mild-tasting fish.

Makes 4 servings

6 orange roughy fillets	Salt and black pepper, to taste
(about 1 pound total)	Milk
Lemon juice (optional)	1 cup one-step stuffing mix
1/2 teaspoon garlic powder	Paprika

Rinse and pat dry fish fillets. Sprinkle with lemon juice, if desired. Arrange fish in a single layer in a 13x9x2-inch glass baking dish. Season with garlic powder, salt and pepper. Add enough milk to come just to top edge of fish. Sprinkle dry stuffing mix on each fillet.

Bake, uncovered, in a preheated 325-degree oven 20 to 30 minutes, or until fish flakes easily when tested with a fork. Remove from oven. Sprinkle paprika on fish. Serve immediately.

Sun Scallops

Jim Hillibish
City Editor, *The Repository*, Canton, OH

Shellfish make excellent eating in record time. That's a big advantage when you must come up with a fine meal in a few minutes. The catch is that it's easy to overcook seafood, so be careful. Sun Scallops is a festive recipe that grew out of a desire to eat healthfully — and quickly. This scallop mixture is delicious served over angel hair pasta. Sun-dried tomatoes, once available only in western states, now are found in most large supermarkets and specialty food stores.

Makes 4 servings

1/4 cup olive oil
5 to 6 sun-dried tomatoes, diced
1 pound bay scallops
1 green onion, minced

1 clove garlic, finely minced
2 teaspoons grated onion
Lime wedges

Heat oil in a large, heavy skillet. (Use a skillet made with a non-reactive metal. Do not use an iron skillet because it will impart an off-taste.) Add dried tomatoes; cook 3 minutes. Add scallops, green onion, garlic and onion. Cook, uncovered, 6 to 8 minutes, or just until scallops turn white. Do not overcook, or scallops will become rubbery. Serve immediately, garnished with wedges of lime.

Never serve alcohol to anyone under the age of 21.

Tuna Casserole Deluxe

Ann Corell Wells
Food Editor, *The Grand Rapids Press*, Grand Rapids, MI

I don't believe there's an American family that didn't grow up on tuna noodle casserole. This recipe, which a friend created many years ago, gives this classic casserole a new twist.

Makes 4 to 6 servings

2 cans (7 1/2 ounces each)
   water-packed tuna,
   drained and flaked
2 cups cooked macaroni
1 cup dairy sour cream
3/4 cup sliced fresh or
   canned mushrooms

1/2 cup sliced black olives
1/4 cup chopped cashews
1/4 teaspoon dried oregano
1/4 to 1/2 cup milk
1/2 cup or more grated
   Cheddar cheese

In a mixing bowl, combine tuna, cooked macaroni, sour cream, mushrooms, olives and cashews. Add enough milk to thin mixture to taste; mix well. Transfer tuna mixture to a lightly greased 1 1/2-quart baking dish. Sprinkle cheese on top. Bake in a preheated 350-degree oven 25 to 30 minutes. Serve hot.

Tuna Medallions with Sesame Seeds

Kasey Wilson
Food Columnist, *The Vancouver Courier*, Vancouver, BC, Canada

All tuna comes from the same family, but the species with the whitest flesh and the most delicate flavor is the most highly prized. The thick coating of sesame seeds in this recipe adds texture, flavor and visual appeal while helping to maintain the juiciness of the fish. Black sesame seeds generally are available in Asian food stores. I like the combination of black and white sesame seeds, but if black ones are not available in your area, use one cup white sesame seeds.

Makes 2 servings

2 fresh tuna medallions
   (4 ounces each)
Salt and freshly ground
   black pepper, to taste
1 cup all-purpose flour
2 eggs, at room temperature,
   separated
1/2 cup black sesame seeds

1/2 cup white sesame seeds
1/2 cup peanut oil or
   vegetable oil
1 teaspoon butter or margarine
1 teaspoon chopped fresh ginger
1/2 cup apple juice
1 cup heavy cream
Fresh cilantro leaves

Season tuna with salt and pepper. Coat tuna pieces with flour, then dip into slightly beaten egg whites. Roll half of each side of the tuna pieces in black sesame seeds and half of each side in white sesame seeds until pieces are completely coated with seeds.

Heat oil in a large, heavy skillet over medium heat; add tuna and gently sauté to medium rare (approximately 5 minutes on each side). Remove tuna from skillet; keep warm in a preheated 200-degree oven. Remove any seeds remaining in the skillet; discard seeds.

Return skillet to medium heat. Add butter; heat until melted. Add ginger; gently cook 2 minutes. Add apple juice and cream; gently cook 2 minutes, stirring occasionally. Remove from heat.

Beat egg yolks; add a small amount of sauce to the yolks and mix well. Add yolk mixture to sauce; mix well. Return skillet to heat; cook about 2 minutes, or until sauce is thickened but not boiling.

Spoon sauce onto 2 serving plates; arrange tuna in the center of each plate. Garnish with cilantro.

Encourage teenagers to call home for a ride if their driver has been drinking.

Tuna Steaks Provençale

Constance Hay
Free-Lance Food Writer, Columbia, MD

Fish has become so popular, I am always searching for simple, yet different, ways to serve it to company. A dish in a restaurant inspired me to create this recipe, which is elegant, colorful and light. My friends and family have enjoyed the result. The tuna steaks can be grilled outdoors in good weather or broiled indoors on days when the weather makes everyone long to be in the south of France. The pimento sauce can be served chilled in the summer or heated in the winter.

Makes 4 servings

1 jar (4 ounces) pimentos, undrained
2 teaspoons anchovy paste
1 clove garlic, minced
1/2 cup reduced-fat sour cream
1 tablespoon caper liquid
2 tablespoons olive oil, divided
1 green bell pepper, cut into strips
1 red bell pepper, cut into strips
1 yellow bell pepper, cut into strips
3/4 cup pimento-stuffed green olives
2 tablespoons capers
4 fresh tuna steaks (6 ounces each)
Salt and black pepper, to taste

In container of food processor or electric blender, combine pimentos with their liquid, anchovy paste and garlic; purée. Add sour cream and caper liquid; mix until well blended. Reserve pimento sauce.

Heat 1 tablespoon oil in a large skillet over medium heat. Add green, red and yellow bell peppers; sauté 2 minutes. Cover; reduce heat and cook 2 minutes. Add olives and capers; heat thoroughly.

Brush tuna steaks on both sides with remaining 1 tablespoon oil. Season with salt and pepper. Broil or grill 4 inches from heat source, turning once. Test tuna with a fork for doneness. When it begins to flake easily and is still moist, remove from broiler or grill. Do not overcook. Total broiling time will be approximately 5 minutes per side for 1-inch-thick tuna steaks.

To serve, spoon a few tablespoons of pimento sauce on each plate; arrange tuna steak on sauce on each plate; ladle tri-color pepper mixture over tuna.

Tuna Steaks with Tomatillo Salsa

Caroline Stuart
Free-Lance Writer, Greenwich, CT

There's nothing easier than cooking on the grill or using the broiler for fast, effortless dinners. This recipe calls for tuna, but any firm-fleshed fish will do. Tomatillos resemble small green tomatoes and have a husk that must be removed before using. They are available in Hispanic markets and many supermarkets. Tomatillos are a popular ingredient in Mexican salsas. This salsa can be prepared ahead of time. Simple grilled tuna with salsa makes an attractive and healthful combination.

Makes 4 servings

8 tomatillos, husks removed, coarsely chopped
2 tomatoes, peeled, seeded, coarsely chopped
2 shallots, minced
2 cloves garlic, minced
1/2 cup plus 2 tablespoons olive oil, divided
3 tablespoons chopped fresh cilantro

1 tablespoon fresh lime juice
Salt and freshly ground black pepper, to taste
1 to 2 fresh chili peppers, to taste, seeded and minced (optional)
4 fresh tuna steaks (8 ounces each)

In a small bowl, combine tomatillos, tomatoes, shallots, garlic, 1/2 cup olive oil, cilantro and lime juice. Season with salt and pepper. Add chili peppers, if desired. Refrigerate salsa until 1 hour before serving, then bring to room temperature before using.

Brush tuna steaks with remaining 2 tablespoons oil. Broil or grill 4 inches from heat source, turning once, about 5 minutes on each side, or until tuna begins to flake easily and is still moist. Do not overcook.

Serve each tuna steak with 4 to 6 tablespoons tomatillo salsa.

Never ride with an alcohol-impaired driver — no matter how old you are.

Poultry

62 Aztec Chili

63 Chicken à l'Orange

64 Chicken à la Mode

65 Chicken Breast Roasted with Spinach and Cheese

66 Chicken Italiano

67 Chicken Madrid

68 Chicken with Hoisin Sauce

69 Easy Chicken Tetrazzini

70 Easy Crispy Chicken

71 Elegantly Easy Chicken

72 Greenbrier Chicken Salad

73 Herbed Turkey Breast

74 Hotshot Chicken

75 Inside-Out Chicken

76 Jalapeño Chicken Curls

77 Mock Stir-Fry

78 Moo-Goo-Gai-Pan Fajitas

79 Plum-Glazed Cornish Hens

80 Provençale Chicken

81 Raspberry Chicken

82 Roasted Cornish Hens

83 Savory Chicken Breasts

84 Shanghai Chicken

85 Turkey Black Bean Chili

86 Turkey Fried Rice

87 Turkey Sausage Italiano

88 White Chili

Aztec Chili

Paula M. Galusha
Free-Lance Home Economist, Tulsa, OK

Ground turkey can be used in many ways, such as in chili or spaghetti sauce. There are as many variations of chili as there are cooks, but this is one of our favorites because it is so fast. It's great for camping trips, too.

Makes 6 servings

2 tablespoons vegetable oil
1/2 cup chopped onion
1 clove garlic, minced
1 pound ground turkey
2 teaspoons chili powder
1 teaspoon salt
1 teaspoon paprika
2 cans (15 1/2 ounces each)
   red kidney beans, undrained

1 can (14 1/2 or 15 ounces)
   stewed tomatoes, undrained
1 can (6 ounces) tomato paste
1/2 teaspoon granulated sugar
1 can (12 ounces) whole
   kernel corn, drained
Hot cooked rice (optional)

Heat oil in 5-quart Dutch oven. Add onion and garlic; cook until onion is tender. Add ground turkey, chili powder, salt and paprika. Cook, stirring often, until turkey is no longer pink.

Drain kidney beans, reserving 1/2 cup liquid. Stir 1/2 cup bean liquid, tomatoes with their liquid, tomato paste and sugar into turkey mixture; mix well. Simmer 30 minutes. Add kidney beans and corn; simmer 15 minutes, stirring occasionally. Serve with rice, if desired.

Make a personal pledge to never drink and drive.

Chicken à l'Orange

Barbara Yost
Feature Writer, *The Phoenix Gazette*, Phoenix, AZ

Isn't it a treat to dine on Duck à l'Orange at the finest restaurant? For those of us with Perrier tastes and tap water budgets, this is a lovely substitute. The orange juice flavors both the rice and the chicken, and keeps the chicken wonderfully moist. For a pretty presentation, add a garnish of thin orange slices and sprinkle a few almonds on top.

Makes 4 to 6 servings

1 1/2 tablespoons butter or
  margarine
3 chicken breasts, skinned,
  boned and halved
3 1/3 cups orange juice

1 teaspoon garlic powder
1 teaspoon dry mustard
Salt and black pepper, to taste
1 1/2 cups uncooked
  long-grain rice

Melt butter in a large skillet. Add chicken breast halves; cook until lightly browned on all sides. Add orange juice, garlic powder, dry mustard, salt and pepper; mix well. Bring mixture to a boil. Add rice. Reduce heat; simmer, covered, 25 minutes, or until rice has absorbed liquid and chicken is done.

Chicken à la Mode

Leona Carlson
Food Writer (Retired), *Rockford Register Star*, Rockford, IL

> *This recipe is fashioned expressly for today's army of cholesterol-counters in a hurry. It's easy to prepare, quick to cook, richly flavored with garlic and basil, and virtually devoid of fat. As a member of that army myself, I can vouch for all these attributes. To make the entire meal low in fat, serve the chicken with a baked potato and a green vegetable, or with pasta tossed with just a dash of olive oil and a garden salad.*

Makes 2 servings

1 chicken breast, skinned, boned and halved

4 tablespoons fat-free Italian dressing

4 thin (about ¼-inch) slices tomato

2 teaspoons dry Italian bread crumbs

1 teaspoon chopped fresh basil

1 teaspoon grated Parmesan cheese (optional)

Combine chicken and Italian dressing in a bowl or plastic bag. Let marinate in refrigerator 2 hours.

Transfer chicken and marinade to a shallow baking pan. Bake, uncovered, in a preheated 400-degree oven 10 minutes.

Top chicken with tomato slices, bread crumbs and basil. Sprinkle Parmesan cheese over all. Return to oven and bake, covered, about 10 minutes. Uncover; bake 10 to 15 minutes, or until chicken is done.

Please remember to say, "No, thanks" to drinks if you're driving.

Chicken Breast Roasted with Spinach and Cheese

Susan Manlin Katzman
Free-Lance Food Writer, St. Louis, MO

Quick and easy means one thing when cooking a weekday, after-work, family meal and quite another when cooking for weekend company. This is a quick-and-easy, perfect-for-company recipe with great versatility. It's as good hot as it is cold and can be served as a dinner or fancy luncheon entrée. Best of all, the dish can be assembled in the cook's spare time, then refrigerated and cooked prior to serving.

Makes 6 to 8 servings

1/2 pound fresh spinach
1 cup ricotta cheese (8 ounces)
1 1/2 cups coarsely grated
   Gouda or Edam cheese
   (about 6 ounces)
3 teaspoons Dijon-style
   mustard, divided

1 1/2 teaspoons chopped
   fresh tarragon
   (or 3/4 teaspoon dried)
Salt and cracked black pepper
4 chicken breasts, boned,
   with skin intact
Vegetable oil

Rinse spinach in cold running water; drain and dry. Remove coarse stems and chop tender leaves. In a large mixing bowl, combine spinach, ricotta cheese, Gouda cheese, 2 teaspoons mustard, tarragon, 1/2 teaspoon salt and pepper to taste. Beat with an electric mixer until ingredients are well blended.

Divide spinach mixture into 4 portions. Loosen the skin of one chicken breast. Stuff one portion spinach mixture under the skin of the breast, spreading mixture as evenly as possible over top of breast. Smooth skin over spinach mixture and gently tuck skin and flesh under to form a neat, plump bundle. Repeat with remaining spinach mixture and chicken breasts.

Oil a large roasting pan; place stuffed chicken in pan, seam-side down. Combine remaining 1 teaspoon mustard and 2 tablespoons vegetable oil; use to coat chicken pieces. Season chicken with salt and pepper. Bake in a preheated 350-degree oven 50 minutes, or until chicken is done.

To serve hot, let chicken stand 10 minutes, then slice crosswise into 1/2-inch thick pieces.

To serve chilled, let chicken cool to room temperature, then wrap and refrigerate. Slice cold chicken crosswise into 1/2-inch thick pieces.

Chicken Italiano

Barbara Mihalevich Arciero
Free-Lance Food Writer, Sacramento, CA

This is a perfect make-it-quick entrée that takes about 30 minutes from start to finish. My family and friends love it. In the unlikely event that there are leftovers, the chicken is just as good cold. The recipe comes from Linda Lucas Dupourque, a busy career woman who has dinner guests at her Wilton, Conn., home at least once a week. This is one of her favorite entrées, too.

Makes 4 servings

½ cup freshly grated Parmesan cheese	¼ teaspoon freshly ground black pepper, or more to taste
2 tablespoons minced fresh parsley	2 chicken breasts, boned, skinned and halved
1 teaspoon dried oregano	2 to 3 tablespoons butter or margarine, melted
1 clove garlic, minced	

In a shallow bowl, combine cheese, parsley, oregano, garlic and pepper; mix well. Dip chicken pieces in melted butter, then in cheese mixture. Place chicken in a shallow baking dish. Drizzle remaining butter over chicken. Bake in a preheated 375-degree oven 25 minutes, or until tender.

Help problem drinkers get expert advice for their difficulties.

Chicken Madrid

Janet Geissler
Food Editor, *Lansing State Journal*, Lansing, MI

I buy bags of frozen, skinned and boned chicken breasts in bulk, so I always have a ready supply in the freezer. The chicken pieces thaw quickly and are the basis for many of my favorite recipes. Here's one quick and easy way to turn plain chicken breasts into a tasty entrée.

Makes 6 servings

3 tablespoons butter or margarine
6 chicken breast halves, skinned
   and boned
1 medium red onion, thinly sliced
   and separated
1 medium green bell pepper,
   cut into thin strips

1 medium red bell pepper,
   cut into thin strips
1 clove garlic, minced
1 can (16 ounces) stewed
   tomatoes, undrained
1/4 cup chopped fresh basil
   or parsley

Melt butter in a large skillet over medium-high heat; add chicken pieces and brown on both sides. Remove chicken from skillet and reserve. Add onion, green and red bell peppers and garlic to skillet. Cook, stirring constantly, until onion slices are transparent. Return reserved chicken to skillet. Add tomatoes with their liquid. Reduce heat to medium-low; simmer, covered, 15 minutes, or until chicken is tender. Top with basil and serve at once.

Chicken with Hoisin Sauce

Delia A. Hammock
Nutrition and Fitness Editor, *Good Housekeeping*, New York, NY

This is a recipe I developed for a cooking class I taught at New York University. Other vegetables, such as water chestnuts, bamboo shoots, broccoli florets or green onions, can be substituted for the red bell pepper and snow peas. When I'm really in a hurry, I pick up pre-washed and pre-cut vegetables from the supermarket salad bar.

Makes 4 servings

1 pound skinned, boned
    chicken breasts
1 1/2 tablespoons soy sauce
1/4 teaspoon crushed red pepper
3 tablespoons hoisin sauce,
    divided (available in Oriental
    food store or international
    section of supermarket)
1 tablespoon vegetable oil
1 tablespoon minced fresh ginger
1 clove garlic, minced

1 medium red bell pepper,
    cut into 3/4-inch pieces
1/4 pound snow peas, stems
    and strings removed
1/4 cup chicken broth
1 teaspoon cornstarch
1 tablespoon cold water
3 ounces roasted,
    unsalted cashews
3 cups hot cooked rice

Cut chicken into 3/4-inch pieces. In a medium bowl, combine soy sauce, crushed red pepper and 2 tablespoons hoisin sauce. Add chicken pieces to soy sauce mixture; stir to coat chicken. Set aside.

In a wok or large skillet, heat oil over high heat. Add ginger and garlic. Stir-fry a few seconds, or until lightly browned. Add the chicken with the marinade; stir-fry 3 to 5 minutes, or until chicken becomes opaque. Add bell pepper and snow peas; stir-fry 1 to 2 minutes. Stir in chicken broth and remaining 1 tablespoon hoisin sauce. Heat quickly. Reduce heat to medium. Cook, covered, 2 minutes, or until vegetables are just tender-crisp.

Combine cornstarch and water; add to chicken mixture. Cook, stirring, until sauce thickens. Stir in cashews. Serve over hot cooked rice.

Ask bars, restaurants and arenas to sponsor Designated Driver programs.

Easy Chicken Tetrazzini

Janet Geissler
Food Editor, *Lansing State Journal*, Lansing, MI

This recipe is one of my favorite ways to use up leftover chicken or turkey. It's a post-Thanksgiving tradition at my house. Although it's a snap to prepare with ingredients you probably have on hand, it tastes rich and elegant. It can be prepared ahead of time and refrigerated until you're ready to pop it into the oven.

Makes 4 to 6 servings

6 to 8 ounces uncooked spaghetti
2 to 3 cups chopped cooked
   chicken or turkey
1 can (10 3/4 ounces) condensed
   cream of mushroom soup,
   undiluted

1/3 cup grated Parmesan cheese
1 can (4 ounces) sliced
   mushrooms, drained
1 cup dairy sour cream
Additional grated Parmesan
   cheese (optional)

Cook spaghetti in boiling water 8 minutes; drain well. In a large mixing bowl, combine cooked spaghetti, cooked chicken, mushroom soup, 1/3 cup Parmesan cheese and mushrooms; mix well. Stir in sour cream.

Transfer spaghetti mixture to a greased 2-quart baking dish. Bake in a preheated 350-degree oven 30 minutes. Before serving, sprinkle with additional Parmesan cheese, if desired.

Easy Crispy Chicken

Marion Riedl
Editorial Staff Writer, *Ludington Daily News*, Ludington, MI

This is a quick-to-fix main dish that can be adjusted to serve one or two, a family or a large group. The first time I prepared this recipe, I was a staff aide at a camp. We prepared it assembly-line style because there were 100-plus girls to feed at the camp. Since that time, I have prepared Easy Crispy Chicken often for my family.

Makes 4 to 6 servings

1 chicken (2 1/2 to 3 pounds),
    cut up (or equivalent amount
    in specific pieces)
About 1 cup butter or
    margarine, melted

About 2 cups crispy rice cereal,
    slightly crushed

Rinse chicken pieces; pat dry with paper towels. Dip chicken pieces in melted butter, then in cereal to coat. Place chicken pieces on a foil-lined baking sheet (the foil is for easy clean-up). Bake in a preheated 350-degree oven 45 to 60 minutes, or until chicken is tender and golden brown.

Note: To estimate amounts when varying the number of servings, allow approximately 1/2 cup butter or margarine and 1 cup crispy rice cereal for 4 pieces of chicken.

Select a Designated Driver when your outing will involve alcohol.

Elegantly Easy Chicken

Sally Scherer
Writer, *The Macon Telegraph*, Macon, GA

Elegantly Easy Chicken is just what it says it is. The curry, apricot preserves and mustard make an elegant, tangy sauce for an easy and quick chicken dish. Although this recipe only serves four, it's easy to add more chicken and more sauce to serve a larger crowd. The chicken is perfect with a green vegetable and warm rolls.

Makes 4 servings

1 jar (12 ounces) apricot preserves
¼ cup Dijon-style mustard
1 teaspoon curry powder
4 skinned, boned chicken breast
    halves (4 ounces each)

1 cup finely chopped, lightly
    salted cashews

In a small saucepan, combine apricot preserves, mustard and curry powder. Cook over low heat, stirring constantly, until preserves are melted.

Dip chicken in apricot mixture, then roll in cashews. Place chicken in a greased 15x10x2-inch baking pan. Bake in a preheated 375-degree oven 15 to 20 minutes, or until chicken is done. Bring remaining sauce to a boil. Serve sauce with chicken.

Greenbrier Chicken Salad

Barbara Gibbs Ostmann
Food Writer, St. Louis, MO

The Greenbrier is one of this country's most famous resorts. Nestled in the beautiful Allegheny Mountains at White Sulphur Springs, West Virginia, the plantation-like resort is a delightful combination of old-fashioned charm and modern convenience. The Greenbrier was the site for a seminar on "Chicken: An American Tradition," at which I sampled many chicken dishes, including this chicken salad that is a perennial favorite on the Greenbrier menu. For ease of preparation, break the recipe into two steps. Poach the chickens on the back burner while fixing dinner one night, then refrigerate the diced meat and assemble the chicken salad the next day. At the Greenbrier, the cooks use homemade mayonnaise, but a good-quality store-bought mayonnaise works well.

Makes 8 servings

2 chickens (2 1/2 pounds each)
1 cup diced celery
2/3 cup dairy sour cream
1 1/3 cups mayonnaise

2 tablespoons white wine vinegar
Salt and freshly ground black
    pepper, to taste

Put chickens in a large stockpot; add lightly salted cold water to cover. Bring to a boil; reduce heat to a simmer. Poach gently, skimming off any foam, 50 to 60 minutes, or until meat is tender when pierced with a knife.

Let chickens cool in poaching liquid until cool enough to handle. Remove chickens from liquid, saving chicken broth for another use. (Broth can be frozen.) Use a paring knife and your fingers to remove all meat from chickens. Discard skin, fat and gristle. Cut meat into 1/2-inch cubes. Refrigerate cubed chicken up to 24 hours before assembling chicken salad.

Combine cubed cooked chicken, diced celery, sour cream, mayonnaise and vinegar; mix gently. Season to taste with salt and pepper. Refrigerate until well chilled before serving.

Serve chicken salad with greens and vegetables as a salad, on bread for a sandwich, or mounded in the hollow of a cantaloupe half.

Never let friends or relatives drink and drive.

Herbed Turkey Breast

Jeanne Voltz
Cookbook Author, Pittsboro, NC

Turkey breast coated with a mixture of fresh herbs cooks in minutes in a hot skillet. The turkey makes an excellent low-fat entrée, served with rice or potatoes and a green vegetable. Turkey cooked this way also is an interesting ingredient in a main-dish salad with greens and other vegetables or fruits.

Makes 4 to 5 servings

2 teaspoons salt
2 teaspoons granulated sugar
1 1/4 pounds turkey breast
   tenderloin
1/4 cup finely sliced green onions
   (green and white parts)
2 tablespoons minced fresh
   thyme or cilantro
2 cloves garlic, minced

1 tablespoon finely grated fresh
   ginger (or 1 teaspoon
   ground ginger)
1 teaspoon coarsely ground
   black pepper
1 teaspoon grated lime peel
3 teaspoons olive oil, or as needed
Lime wedges
Sprigs of fresh thyme or cilantro

Combine salt and sugar on a plate; rub thoroughly into the turkey. Place turkey in a bowl or plastic bag; refrigerate 2 to 3 hours.

In a small bowl, combine green onions, thyme, garlic, ginger, pepper and lime peel. Mix well; set aside.

Remove turkey from refrigerator; rinse off as much salt-sugar mixture as possible. Pat turkey dry with paper towels. Cut turkey into 4 or 5 serving pieces. Place turkey pieces between two sheets of plastic wrap; pound to 1/2-inch thickness with a flat mallet, flat side of a heavy knife or rim of a saucer. Coat turkey pieces with reserved green onion mixture, pressing it firmly onto the turkey meat.

Heat 2 teaspoons of the oil in a large skillet. Add turkey in a single layer, taking care not to crowd the pan. Cook until brown on both sides. Reduce heat; cook until thoroughly done. Add remaining oil, if needed. Total cooking time is about 6 minutes.

Place turkey pieces on a serving platter or individual plates. Garnish with lime wedges and thyme sprigs.

Hotshot Chicken

Narcisse S. Cadgène
Free-Lance Writer, New York, NY

I've fooled a lot of people with this simple dish. The sauce tastes as though I've spent hours in the kitchen using tons of different ingredients. Wrong! This simple recipe takes two minutes to throw together from ingredients most of us have on hand at all times. So far, no friend of mine has been able to guess that two store-bought condiments make up most of this tangy sauce. You can vary the spiciness by using mild, medium or hot salsa or taco sauce.

Makes 4 to 6 servings

1/2 cup chunky salsa or
    chunky taco sauce
    (mild, medium or hot)
1/4 cup Dijon-style mustard
Juice of 1 lime

3 chicken breasts, skinned,
    boned and halved
2 to 4 tablespoons vegetable oil
3 tablespoons heavy cream

In a large non-reactive bowl, combine salsa, mustard and lime juice; mix well. Pound each chicken breast half lightly to flatten the thickest part so the pieces will cook more evenly. Add chicken pieces to salsa mixture, turning each piece to coat. If you have time, let chicken marinate at least 30 minutes or refrigerate overnight.

To cook, heat oil in a large skillet over medium heat. Shake excess salsa mixture from each piece of chicken. Add chicken to skillet; cook chicken, turning once after about 10 minutes.

When chicken is browned and just cooked through, add remaining salsa mixture to skillet. Cook 3 to 4 minutes, turning chicken pieces to coat with salsa mixture. When the salsa mixture begins to glaze slightly, drizzle cream over the chicken, shaking pan to distribute cream. Cook 1 minute to heat cream.

Place chicken on a warm serving platter or individual plates. Ladle sauce over chicken. Serve immediately.

Keep a MADD/Family Vacation Pack in your car.

Inside-Out Chicken

Beth Whitley Duke
Food Editor, *Amarillo Globe-News*, Amarillo, TX

Most people think of putting stuffing inside a chicken. This recipe turns that idea inside out by using the stuffing as a coating for the chicken. The end result is crunchy, baked chicken — a versatile main dish prepared with a minimum of effort. If there is any chicken left over, it tastes just as good the next day cold from the refrigerator.

Makes 6 to 8 servings

About 2 cups
   herb-seasoned stuffing mix
   (or coarse dry bread crumbs)

8 to 10 chicken breast halves
1 cup prepared Italian oil
   and vinegar salad dressing

Use a food processor or electric blender to crush dry stuffing mix into coarse crumbs. Transfer stuffing crumbs to a shallow bowl. Dip chicken pieces in salad dressing, then roll chicken in stuffing crumbs, coating all sides.

Place chicken, skin-side up, in a well-greased shallow baking pan that is large enough to hold all the chicken pieces with space between the pieces. Moisten any remaining stuffing crumbs with remaining salad dressing; use to fill spaces between chicken pieces. Bake in a preheated 350-degree oven 1 hour, or until chicken is tender.

Microwave directions: Put breaded chicken in one layer in a well-greased microwave-safe baking dish. Cover with waxed paper or paper towels. Microwave on High (100 percent) power 15 to 18 minutes. Rotate dish 1/2 turn halfway through microwaving time. Let stand 2 to 3 minutes, uncovered, before serving.

Jalapeño Chicken Curls

Beth Whitley Duke
Food Editor, *Amarillo Globe-News*, Amarillo, TX

Jalapeños (pronounced hal-ah-pain-yas) are the small green chili peppers used in Tex-Mex cooking that look so innocent on the plate yet conceal a taste hotter than a rancher's branding iron. The best quote I know about peppers came from the chief pepper buyer at the Pace Picante Sauce Co. in San Antonio, Texas. He said, "Peppers are like spouses. You never know what you've got until it's too late!"

This recipe tucks a jalapeño (or half of one, for starters) inside a cream cheese-filled chicken breast to make an elegant main dish that is a few degrees above the normal. Add a green salad, tostado chips and Spanish rice for a complete meal.

Makes 6 servings

3 large chicken breasts, skinned,
  boned and halved
1 tablespoon butter or
  margarine, softened
1 container (8 ounces) whipped
  cream cheese with chives,
  at room temperature

6 fresh or canned jalapeños
6 slices bacon

Flatten chicken breast halves to 1/2-inch thickness by hammering them with a kitchen mallet. Spread butter on each chicken piece, then spread about 3 tablespoons cream cheese on each. Place a jalapeño at the edge of the cheese-topped side, then roll up chicken piece around the jalapeño (with the cheese on the inside of the roll). Repeat with remaining chicken pieces and jalapeños.

(If your family likes spicy food, use a whole jalapeño, seeds and all, discarding only the stem. For a medium version, remove seeds from the jalapeño. For a mild version, use half of a seeded jalapeño.)

Wrap a slice of bacon around each chicken roll. Place rolls, seam-side down, in a shallow baking dish. Bake in a preheated 400-degree oven 40 minutes, or until chicken is tender. Complete cooking by broiling 5 minutes, or until bacon is crisp.

Read your local MADD chapter newsletter.

Mock Stir-Fry

Monetta L. Harr
Food Editor, *Jackson Citizen Patriot*, Jackson, MI

This recipe is the result of a trip to the supermarket with my husband, Jerry, one winter afternoon. We wanted to come up with something tasty yet different and easy to make for our family's dinner. My husband has always loved okra, and he decided to build a dish around that. It has remained a favorite with our family. The beauty of this dish is that you can substitute any canned vegetable for the okra or green beans. If you want to add chopped onion, celery or green pepper, that's perfectly fine if you don't mind an extra step. Likewise, a sprinkling of mozzarella cheese at the end of the cooking process would be good, too. The basic recipe is fast, easy and nutritious, and clean-up is minimal. We serve the stir-fry over rice, along with a salad and garlic toast.

Makes 6 servings

1 1/2 pounds ground turkey
1 teaspoon garlic powder
1 teaspoon salt
1/2 teaspoon black pepper
2 cans (14 1/2 ounces each) Italian-style stewed tomatoes, undrained
1 can (14 1/2 ounces) okra, undrained

1 can (16 ounces) green beans, drained
1 can (8 ounces) mushroom pieces, drained
1 teaspoon beef bouillon granules (optional)
Hot cooked rice

In an electric skillet or in a large skillet on top of the stove, combine ground turkey, garlic powder, salt and pepper; mix well. Cook until turkey is brown. Add tomatoes with their liquid, okra with liquid, green beans, mushrooms and bouillon granules; mix well. Simmer, covered, 20 to 30 minutes, stirring occasionally. Serve over rice.

Moo-Goo-Gai-Pan Fajitas

Carolyn Flournoy
Food Columnist, *The Times*, Shreveport, LA

My daughter and her roommates at graduate school existed on Chinese take-out food. My sons, on the other hand, favored any Mexican dish put before them. I solved the global cuisine problem at home with what we call Moo-Goo-Gai-Pan Fajitas. They're easy to prepare and you can vary the ingredients to fit what's in your pantry or the refrigerator. If you prefer corn tortillas to flour, use them instead.

Makes 8 servings

1 tablespoon butter or margarine
2 eggs, beaten
1/4 teaspoon garlic powder
2 tablespoons peanut oil
1 carrot, sliced diagonally
1 pound skinned, boned chicken
    breasts, cut into 1-inch pieces
1 cup picante sauce

2 cups shredded cabbage
1 can (8 ounces) bamboo shoots,
    drained
6 green onions, cut into 1-inch
    pieces (green and white parts)
1 teaspoon lemon juice
8 flour tortillas, warmed

Melt butter in a large skillet. Add eggs and garlic powder; cook, stirring with a fork, until eggs are done. Remove scrambled egg mixture from skillet; keep warm.

In the same skillet, heat oil. Add carrot; cook just until tender-crisp. Remove carrot from skillet; keep warm.

Add chicken to skillet; cook, stirring constantly, until chicken is brown on all sides. Add picante sauce; blend well. Simmer, uncovered, 5 minutes. Add reserved egg mixture, reserved cooked carrot, cabbage, bamboo shoots, green onions and lemon juice; mix well. Cook, uncovered, 2 minutes.

Put a portion of chicken mixture in the center of each tortilla; roll up. Serve with extra picante sauce, if desired.

Learn more about MADD's Speakers Bureau.

Plum-Glazed Cornish Hens

Stacy Lam
Reporter, *The Macon Telegraph*, Macon, GA

I'm always looking for something different to grill, and this is one of the more unusual ideas I've found. It makes an elegant meal from the grill. I found the recipe on a calendar several years ago. This recipe and several others are so good I'll probably always keep that 1989 calendar.

Makes 4 servings

2 Cornish game hens	2 tablespoons ketchup
(1 1/2 pounds each)	1 tablespoon soy sauce
2 tablespoons butter or	1/2 teaspoon ground ginger
margarine, melted	1/2 teaspoon granulated sugar
1/2 cup plum preserves	

Cut each Cornish hen in half; rinse and pat dry with paper towels. Brush hen pieces with melted butter. Place pieces, skin-side up, on grill rack over hot coals. Grill, covered, about 15 minutes. Turn; grill, covered, 15 minutes, or until fork-tender.

Meanwhile, combine plum preserves, ketchup, soy sauce, ginger and sugar in a small bowl; mix well. Brush sauce on hen pieces during the last 5 minutes of cooking. Serve remaining sauce with the hens.

Provençale Chicken

Janet Geissler
Food Editor, *Lansing State Journal*, Lansing, MI

Here is a simple and speedy dish that's a complete meal — chicken, vegetables and pasta all cooked together. Provençale Chicken combines the flavors of the Old World with the convenience busy Americans have come to expect. I like to serve this with a salad made of sliced oranges and onions with a vinaigrette dressing.

Makes 4 servings

1 tablespoon olive oil
1/2 teaspoon minced garlic
2 cans (16 ounces each) tomatoes, undrained, broken up
2 cans (6 3/4 ounces each) chunk chicken breast, undrained

1 package (9 ounces) frozen Italian green beans, thawed
3/4 cup pitted black olives
2 teaspoons dried basil
2 cups uncooked egg noodles

Heat oil in a large skillet. Add garlic; cook over medium-high heat 1 minute, or until golden brown. Add tomatoes with their liquid, canned chicken with liquid, green beans, olives and basil; stir to mix. Add egg noodles; gently stir until noodles are covered with liquid. Bring mixture to a boil; reduce heat. Cover and simmer, stirring occasionally, 8 to 10 minutes, or until noodles are tender.

MADD needs your help to stop drinking and driving.

Raspberry Chicken

Dorothy Cunningham
Free-Lance Writer, Morenci, MI

I first tasted this raspberry-sauced chicken at a dinner party. Anticipating my request, the hostess had a copy of the recipe typed and ready for me. Because she is always busy with her three children and a full-time job, she relies on this quick-to-fix chicken dish to wow her friends. It works! It takes less than 30 minutes to prepare, from start to finish, yet it tastes as though you spent hours in the kitchen.

Makes 4 servings

2 large chicken breasts, skinned, boned and halved (about 3/4 pound meat)
Salt, to taste
2 tablespoons butter or margarine
1/4 cup finely chopped onion

3 tablespoons raspberry jelly (or plum jelly)
3 tablespoons white vinegar
1 tablespoon brown sugar
1/4 cup heavy cream

Cut the 4 chicken breast halves in half lengthwise, to make 8 pieces. Lightly salt chicken pieces. Melt butter in a 10-inch skillet. Add chicken; cook over medium heat 5 minutes. Turn chicken. Add onion around edges of skillet. Cook 5 to 10 minutes, or until chicken is done. Transfer chicken to a platter; keep warm.

Add jelly, vinegar and brown sugar to mixture remaining in skillet. Cook over high heat, scraping up bits in the pan. Bring to a boil; boil 1 minute, or until sauce is slightly reduced. Let cool slightly; stir in cream. Heat just to boiling. Pour sauce over chicken. Serve immediately.

Note: Scatter a few fresh or frozen raspberries over the sauced chicken for a gourmet garnish.

Roasted Cornish Hens

Toni Burks
Food Editor, *Roanoke Times & World-News*, Roanoke, VA

The trendsetters tell us that at-home dinner parties are in. For some of us, though, inviting company to share a great meal has never been out of fashion. Roasted Cornish Hens are ideal for these occasions because they're elegant and easy — for an accomplished cook as well as the novice.

Makes 8 servings

4 Cornish game hens
   (1 to 1 1/2 pounds each)
Salt and black pepper, to taste
Onion powder, to taste

1/2 cup butter or margarine
1/4 cup chicken broth
1/2 cup orange marmalade

Use kitchen shears to cut away backbone of Cornish hens. Spread hens out flat on cutting board; use a sharp knife to split each hen in half. Rinse Cornish hen pieces; pat dry with paper towels. Sprinkle pieces with salt, black pepper and onion powder. Arrange pieces skin-side up, in a shallow roasting pan.

In small saucepan, combine butter, chicken broth and marmalade. Cook, stirring, over medium heat until mixture is well blended. Pour mixture evenly over hen pieces in pan.

Bake in a preheated 325-degree oven 1 to 1 1/2 hours, or until done; baste often with marmalade mixture. Add more chicken broth, if necessary. Serve hens with sauce from the roasting pan.

Ask your friends and family to pledge to be safe and sober drivers.

Savory Chicken Breasts

Florence Larson
Food Editor, *Norfolk Daily News*, Norfolk, NE

The following recipe was given to me several years ago. I have used it numerous times for family dinners and guests, and it is always a hit. Serve the chicken with either rice or noodles; my family prefers noodles, but either is good. The recipe can be doubled successfully.

Makes 4 to 6 servings

2 tablespoons butter or margarine
3 chicken breasts, boned,
   skinned and halved
3 carrots, thinly sliced
1 can (10 3/4 ounces) condensed
   cream of chicken soup,
   undiluted

1/4 cup milk
1/2 teaspoon salt
Black pepper, to taste

Melt butter in a large skillet. Add chicken breast halves; turn to brown all over. Add carrots. In a small bowl, combine cream of chicken soup, milk, salt and pepper; mix well. Pour soup mixture over chicken and carrots. Simmer, covered, 25 to 30 minutes, or until chicken is done and carrots are tender.

Shanghai Chicken

Leona Carlson
Food Writer (Retired), *Rockford Register Star*, Rockford, IL

As an enforced cholesterol-counter, I have become an unintentional expert in chicken- and turkey-breast cuisine. This is one of the best low-fat recipes I have found. It is equally popular with my grandchildren, who, at ages 4 to 9, have limited but well-defined food preferences. The sauce and any chicken leftovers can be refrigerated and reheated.

Makes 4 to 6 servings

2 cloves garlic, minced
1/2 cup soy sauce
Juice of 1 lemon
1/4 cup honey
2 tablespoons paprika
1 1/2 teaspoons dry mustard

Pinch dried thyme
1 chicken (2 1/2 to 3 pounds),
    cut up (or equivalent amount
    of specific pieces)
Hot cooked rice

In a small bowl, combine garlic, soy sauce, lemon juice, honey, paprika, dry mustard and thyme; mix well.

Arrange chicken pieces in a single layer in a 13x9x2-inch baking pan. Pour garlic sauce over chicken. Let marinate in refrigerator 1 hour.

Bake in a preheated 375-degree oven 1 hour, basting every 10 minutes with the garlic sauce in pan. (The basting is important.) Serve with rice.

Note: If you like extra sauce to serve at the table, double the amounts of the garlic sauce ingredients. Refrigerate any leftovers.

Be a responsible host.

Turkey Black Bean Chili

Lori Longbotham
Free-Lance Food Writer, Astoria, NY

Chili doesn't have to be made with beef. This version made with ground turkey is lighter and more healthful than regular chili. It's a terrific recipe to make ahead and have on hand. Toss it together while cooking tonight's meal and have an effortless dinner tomorrow, or double the batch and freeze some for an almost-instant meal when you really need one.

Makes 4 servings

2 tablespoons vegetable oil
1 onion, diced
1 ½ tablespoons chili powder
2 cloves garlic, minced
2 teaspoons ground cumin
1 bay leaf
½ teaspoon anise seeds
½ teaspoon ground coriander
½ pound ground turkey
1 can (16 ounces) whole tomatoes
    in thick purée, undrained
1 can (15 ounces) black beans,
    drained and rinsed

1 red bell pepper, diced
1 to 2 jalapeño peppers,
    seeded and minced
Salt and cayenne pepper, to taste
2 tablespoons minced
    fresh cilantro
Cilantro, plain yogurt or dairy
    sour cream, grated Cheddar
    cheese, minced green onions
    and/or avocado, for garnish

Heat oil in a heavy Dutch oven over medium-high heat. Add onion; cook, stirring occasionally, 5 minutes, or until onion is soft. Add chili powder, garlic, cumin, bay leaf, anise seeds and coriander; mix well. Cook, stirring, 3 minutes. Add ground turkey; cook, stirring occasionally, 5 to 7 minutes, or until pink disappears. Add tomatoes with their liquid, black beans, bell pepper, jalapeños, salt and cayenne. Bring to a boil.

Remove Dutch oven from stovetop and put in preheated 350-degree oven; bake, uncovered, 45 minutes, stirring twice. Stir in cilantro. Serve hot. Pass desired garnishes.

Turkey Fried Rice

Lorrie Guttman
Food Editor, *Tallahassee Democrat*, Tallahassee, FL

My family adores this Americanized stir-fry. It won our newspaper's contest for recipes using ground turkey several years ago, and I've enjoyed it ever since. I did make two changes: I use more vegetables than called for in the original, and I don't use any fat to brown the turkey, because it has enough itself. If you have cooked rice on hand, the recipe is especially quick. Otherwise cook some instant rice while you prepare the first part of the recipe.

Makes 4 servings

1 pound ground turkey
2 eggs, slightly beaten
1 onion, thinly sliced
1 package (16 ounces) frozen
    mixed vegetables, thawed
2 to 4 tablespoons soy sauce,
    or to taste

1 teaspoon black pepper
1 teaspoon ground ginger
Dash cayenne pepper
1 cup cooked brown or
    long-grain rice

Brown ground turkey in a skillet over medium heat. Add eggs; scramble with turkey. Add onion; cook until onion is brown. Add mixed vegetables, soy sauce, pepper, ginger and cayenne; mix well. When vegetables are cooked, add cooked rice. Cook, stirring, until liquid has evaporated and mixture is heated through. Serve at once.

Stop serving drinks at least 90 minutes before the party ends.

Turkey Sausage Italiano

Constance Hay
Free-Lance Food Writer, Columbia, MD

Now there is a way for those who love Italian sausage but must watch their cholesterol levels to have the flavor without the guilt. I serve this cacciatore-style dish over steamed spaghetti squash or lightly sautéed coins of zucchini or yellow crookneck squash for a change from pasta.

Makes 4 to 6 servings

1 pound sweet Italian turkey sausage links	1/4 cup tomato paste
2 teaspoons olive oil	3 tablespoons minced fresh parsley
1 onion, diced	1 teaspoon Italian seasoning
1 can (28 ounces) Italian tomatoes, undrained	1/4 teaspoon black pepper
	2 green bell peppers, diced

In a large skillet, sauté turkey sausage until well browned. Set aside.

Drain any fat from skillet; add olive oil to skillet and heat. Add onion; cook until transparent. Purée tomatoes with their liquid in a food processor or electric blender. Add tomato paste, parsley, Italian seasoning and pepper to puréed tomatoes; mix well. Add tomato mixture to onions in skillet; mix well.

Return sausage links to skillet. Bring mixture to a boil, then reduce heat and simmer rapidly 20 minutes, or until sauce is slightly thickened. Add bell peppers; cook 10 minutes.

Serve sausage and sauce over steamed spaghetti squash or cooked pasta, as desired.

White Chili

Barbara Gibbs Ostmann
Food Writer, St. Louis, MO

Although chili usually features beef and tomatoes and is dark in color, this White Chili calls for cooked turkey, canned green chilies and white kidney beans (cannellini). It might not look like chili at first glance, but just wait until you taste it — it's great! I sampled this at the National Turkey Federation booth at a food media conference and immediately adopted the recipe as one of my own. It's quick and easy to prepare, yet full of Southwestern flavor. Turkey leftovers never tasted so good.

Makes 4 servings

1 tablespoon olive oil
1 ¹/₂ cups coarsely chopped onions
2 cloves garlic, minced
1 jalapeño pepper, minced (fresh or canned; seeded, if desired)
1 can (4 ounces) chopped mild green chilies, drained
1 teaspoon ground cumin
¹/₂ teaspoon dried oregano
¹/₄ teaspoon cayenne pepper

¹/₄ teaspoon salt, or to taste
1 cup chicken broth
1 can (19 ounces) white kidney beans (cannellini), drained and rinsed
2 cups cubed cooked turkey (¹/₂-inch cubes)
¹/₄ cup coarsely chopped fresh cilantro
¹/₂ cup shredded Monterey Jack cheese

Heat oil in a 3-quart saucepan over medium-high heat. Add onions and garlic; sauté 5 minutes, or until onion is tender. Add jalapeño, green chilies, cumin, oregano, cayenne and salt. Cook 1 minute. Stir in broth, beans and cooked turkey. Bring to a boil; reduce heat and simmer, uncovered, 20 to 25 minutes, or until slightly thickened. Stir in cilantro.

To serve, ladle chili into bowls; top each serving with 2 tablespoons cheese.

Note: Substitute cooked chicken for turkey, if desired.

Friends keep friends alive. Don't let your friends drink and drive.

Pork

90 Blue Ribbon Ham Loaf

91 Caribbean Pork

92 Fruit-Glazed Ham

93 Knockwurst and Cabbage

94 Lean Pork Loin with
Onions and Raisins

95 Peasant Pork Chops

96 Pork Chops and Sweet Potatoes

97 Pork Chops, Alsatian Style

98 Pork with Spicy Peanut Sauce

99 Quick Cassoulet

100 Sausage and Peppers

101 Sausage-Stuffed Zucchini

102 Simple Sauté

103 Slightly Cajun Pork Chops

104 Soda Pop Chops

105 Southern Pork Jumble

106 Sugar and Anise Baked Ham

107 Thyme for Pork Chops

108 Warm Pork and Fruit Salad

Blue Ribbon Ham Loaf

Constance Hay
Free-Lance Food Writer, Columbia, MD

My family named this recipe after I won a blue ribbon for it at the Ohio State Fair. It has stood the test of time for its fine flavor, simple ingredients and easy preparation. Most of the work is done by the supermarket butcher. Ask him to grind equal amounts of smoked ham and lean pork. Once the ingredients are mixed and the loaf is formed, it requires no further attention until it is removed from the oven. It can be assembled ahead of time and refrigerated until baking time. For company, surround the ham loaf with parsley and orange slices. You might want to double the recipe because leftovers make delicious sandwiches.

Makes 4 to 6 servings

3/4 pound ground smoked ham
3/4 pound lean ground pork
1 cup buttery-flavor cracker
    crumbs (about 22 round
    crackers, such as Ritz)

1 egg, well beaten
1/2 cup milk

In a mixing bowl, combine ham, pork, cracker crumbs, egg and milk. Mix well. Shape into loaf and place in a 9x9x2-inch baking pan. Bake in a preheated 350-degree oven 75 minutes. Let cool 10 minutes before slicing.

Be a responsible guest. Don't drink to excess at your host's home.

Caribbean Pork

Narcisse S. Cadgène
Free-Lance Writer, New York, NY

Ah, to be in the islands: the long sunny days, the gentle sound of azure waves slapping against perfect white beaches, the fragrant caress of trade winds, a healthful, satisfying meal enjoyed while watching the sun melt into the horizon.... Dear me. Well, at least we can all have the "healthful, satisfying meal" part of this little daydream, and with little time or effort. This recipe is the indoor version. If outdoor grilling is more your style, marinate the pork in the other ingredients, then heat the marinade for use as a basting sauce.

Makes 4 servings

2 tablespoons vegetable oil or
    light olive oil
4 boneless center-cut pork chops
    (3/4-inch thick)
1 medium onion, sliced
1/2 teaspoon dried rosemary

Grated peel of 1 lime
1/4 cup lime juice (about 2 limes)
1/4 teaspoon cayenne pepper,
    or more, to taste
Salt, to taste

Heat oil in a large skillet. Add pork chops; reduce heat to medium. Cook about 3 minutes on one side, or until chops are cooked about halfway through (look at the sides). Turn each chop; move them all toward one side of the skillet.

Place onion slices in the empty side of the skillet. Lower heat slightly; cook 3 to 5 minutes, stirring onions so they cook evenly. Add rosemary, lime peel and lime juice. Cook, turning chops once or twice, until onions are somewhat browned and quite soft, and pork chops have absorbed some of the juices. Season with cayenne and salt. Serve pork chops with cooked onions.

Fruit-Glazed Ham

Barbara Mihalevich Arciero
Free-Lance Food Writer, Sacramento, CA

I spent several years of my childhood living on a small hog farm in Shelbina, Mo. I suppose it goes without saying that my family ate plenty of pork, prepared in nearly every way imaginable. This recipe originated with Jeana Fox, a friend of my mother. It doubles and triples easily, and it's always a hit.

Makes 4 to 6 servings

1 can (20 ounces)
    pineapple chunks
1 can (17 ounces) apricot halves
1/3 cup firmly packed
    brown sugar
2 tablespoons cornstarch

2 tablespoons cider vinegar
1 teaspoon soy sauce
1/4 teaspoon ground ginger
Approximately 3 pounds cooked
    ham, sliced 1 1/2-inches
    thick or cut into chunks

Drain pineapple chunks and apricot halves, reserving juice from both cans. Set fruit aside. Combine juices; add enough water to make 2 cups liquid.

In a saucepan, combine brown sugar and cornstarch; mix well. Stir in 2 cups fruit juice mixture, vinegar, soy sauce and ginger; mix well. Cook over medium heat, stirring constantly, until mixture thickens.

Put ham slices in a 13x9x2-inch baking dish; top with reserved pineapple and reserved apricots. Pour thickened brown sugar mixture over all. Bake, uncovered, in a preheated 350-degree oven 35 minutes, or until very hot.

Help others act responsibly about drinking and driving.

Knockwurst and Cabbage

Toni Burks
Food Editor, *Roanoke Times & World-News*, Roanoke, VA

Fat sausages, heady cabbage and earthy root vegetables make fine fall fare. I like this one-pot meal after a day of leaf raking or after gazing at puffy white clouds skimming over a clear autumn sky. Corn muffins or corn sticks are all that's needed to complete the menu.

Makes 4 servings

4 knockwurst sausages
    (about 1 pound total)
1 tablespoon vegetable oil
1 medium head cabbage,
    coarsely shredded or sliced
1 onion, sliced
1 cup thinly sliced carrots
1 clove garlic, minced

1 pound small red potatoes,
    sliced, unpared
3/4 cup apple juice
3/4 cup water
1 teaspoon chicken
    bouillon granules
1 teaspoon mixed pickling spice
1/2 teaspoon salt

Make 3 slits in each knockwurst. Heat oil in a large, deep skillet or saucepan. Add knockwurst; cook over medium heat until brown. Remove knockwurst from skillet; set aside. Drain excess fat from skillet.

In the same skillet, combine cabbage, onion, carrots and garlic; cook until onion is soft. Add potatoes, apple juice, water, chicken bouillon granules, mixed pickling spice and salt. Simmer, covered, 20 minutes. Stir, then arrange reserved knockwurst on top. Simmer, covered, 10 minutes. Serve hot.

Note: Knockwurst (also spelled knackwurst) are made of pork and/or beef. Any kind will work well in this recipe.

Lean Pork Loin with Onions and Raisins

Lori Longbotham
Free-Lance Food Writer, Astoria, NY

Influenced by Italian cuisine, this simple yet sophisticated dish would be great with a green salad and a cool refreshing beverage for a quick weekday supper. You can have this recipe on the table in less time than it would take to cook a frozen entrée — and this is much tastier and more nutritious.

Makes 2 servings

3 tablespoons chicken broth	2 small onions, thinly sliced
1 tablespoon balsamic vinegar	6 ounces lean boneless pork loin,
1 tablespoon golden raisins	thinly sliced
1/2 teaspoon grated lemon peel	1 tablespoon pine nuts
1 tablespoon olive oil	(pignolia), toasted

In a small bowl, combine chicken broth, vinegar, raisins and lemon peel.

Heat oil in a medium non-stick skillet over medium heat. Add onions; cook, stirring frequently, 7 to 8 minutes, or until lightly browned. Add chicken broth mixture; cook 1 minute, or until broth has almost completely evaporated. Transfer onion mixture to bowl.

In the same skillet, sauté pork slices over medium heat about 1 1/2 minutes, or until browned on both sides. Arrange pork on a serving platter; keep warm.

Pour pan juices and any browned bits from skillet over onion mixture; stir to combine. Spoon onion mixture over pork; sprinkle pine nuts on top. Serve immediately.

Learn the facts about the dangers of drinking and driving.

Peasant Pork Chops

Barbara Fisher
Food Writer, *This Week Publications*, Farmingdale, NY

Armed with the knowledge that pork chops should be thoroughly cooked, I had a tendency to overcook them, which usually produced chops that were dry and tasteless. By changing cooking methods, choosing instead to cook them in liquid, I finally achieved success in my quest for savory pork chops, tender enough to cut with a fork. The gentle moist cooking tenderizes the meat and allows it to absorb the flavor of the liquid which is bolstered by the addition of aromatic vegetables. This recipe is simple to make — it can be prepared in one pot and doesn't require a lot of attention.

Makes 4 servings

2 tablespoons butter or margarine
4 pork chops (1-inch thick),
   trimmed of excess fat
All-purpose flour, for
   dredging chops
1 teaspoon dried thyme

Salt and black pepper, to taste
4 medium carrots, cut diagonally
   into 1-inch pieces
4 large potatoes, quartered
2 large onions, quartered
3 cups beef broth

Melt butter in large skillet or pot. Lightly coat pork chops with flour, then brown chops on both sides in butter. Season chops with thyme, salt and pepper. Add carrots, potatoes, onions and broth to skillet. Simmer, covered, 35 to 40 minutes, or until pork chops are tender.

Pork Chops and Sweet Potatoes

Debra Carr-Elsing
Food Writer, *The Capital Times*, Madison, WI

One-dish meals are a must in our busy household. We all like sweet potatoes, so I paired sweet potatoes with pork chops for an easy one-dish meal.

Makes 4 servings

1 tablespoon vegetable oil
4 pork loin chops (1/2-inch thick)
1 can (20 ounces) pineapple
   chunks in juice
3 tablespoons brown sugar
1/2 teaspoon salt

1/2 teaspoon ground cinnamon
2 medium sweet potatoes, peeled
   and cut into 1-inch pieces
1 medium green bell pepper,
   cut into 1-inch chunks
1 tablespoon cornstarch

Heat oil in a large skillet or Dutch oven. Add pork chops; cook 3 minutes on each side, or until browned. Remove chops from pan and reserve.

Drain pineapple, reserving juice. Add 1/2 cup of the reserved pineapple juice, brown sugar, salt and cinnamon to drippings in the skillet; mix well. Add sweet potatoes; turn to coat with liquid. Return pork chops to skillet. Bring to a boil. Reduce heat to low; simmer, covered, 20 minutes, or until sweet potatoes are tender.

Stir in bell pepper and pineapple chunks. Simmer, covered, 5 minutes. Transfer pork chops to a warm platter.

In a small bowl, combine cornstarch and remaining pineapple juice; mix well. Gradually stir cornstarch mixture into sweet potato mixture in skillet. Cook, stirring, over medium heat until sauce thickens; spoon over pork chops. Serve immediately.

Recognize the signs of the alcohol-impaired driver.

Pork Chops, Alsatian Style

Lori Longbotham
Free-Lance Food Writer, Astoria, NY

This recipe requires little work and little time for lots of flavor and comfort. The result is a homey, family-style meal that's good in any season, but especially on a cold winter evening.

Makes 4 servings

2 tablespoons unsalted butter
1 pound sauerkraut, rinsed
    and drained
1/2 ripe pear, peeled and diced
2 small green onions, minced
    (green and white parts)
1 tablespoon dark brown sugar
1 teaspoon fresh thyme leaves

1/4 teaspoon caraway seeds
1 tablespoon vegetable oil
8 blade pork chops
    (about 1/2-inch thick)
Salt and freshly ground
    black pepper, to taste
1 teaspoon minced fresh parsley

Melt butter in medium skillet over medium heat. Add sauerkraut, pear, green onions, brown sugar, thyme and caraway seeds. Simmer, uncovered, 10 minutes, stirring occasionally.

Meanwhile, heat oil in a large skillet over medium heat. Add pork chops in batches. Cook chops about 3 minutes on each side, or until browned and cooked through. Remove each batch and keep warm. Season chops with salt and pepper.

Drain fat from skillet. Deglaze skillet with the sauerkraut mixture, stirring up any browned bits from bottom of skillet.

Place pork chops on serving plates; top with sauerkraut mixture and garnish with parsley.

Pork with Spicy Peanut Sauce

Narcisse S. Cadgène
Free-Lance Writer, New York, NY

This variation on Indonesian pork saté is especially delicious. Once upon a time we had some left over, and it never even made it to the microwave oven for reheating — I ate it cold and loved it. If I have extra sauce left over, I find myself snitching little bites out of the jar in the refrigerator during the day, too.

Makes 4 servings

1/2 cup sesame oil
1/4 cup creamy peanut butter
1/4 cup soy sauce
3 tablespoons granulated sugar
1 tablespoon minced garlic

1 teaspoon crushed red pepper
2 tablespoons vegetable oil
1 1/4 pounds lean pork loin,
   cut into thin strips

In a small bowl, combine sesame oil, peanut butter, soy sauce, sugar, garlic and crushed red pepper; mix well. If mixture is too thick, warm in a microwave oven or heat on top of the stove. Blend thoroughly.

In a wok or large skillet, heat vegetable oil until quite hot. Add pork; cook, stirring often, just until pork is cooked through and juices run clear. Do not overcook.

Spoon about half the sauce over the pork; cook 30 to 60 seconds to heat thoroughly. Serve at once. Pass remaining sauce at the table.

Note: Sesame oil is available in supermarkets or Asian food markets. If you cannot find it, use 1/2 cup vegetable oil and 1/2 teaspoon toasted sesame seeds.

Protect yourself from injury caused by drunk drivers. Always wear your seat belt.

Quick Cassoulet

Mary Beth Jung
Free-Lance Food Writer, Grafton, WI

The traditional version of this French country dish requires hours to prepare. This quick version incorporates convenience foods for a cassoulet that is ready to serve in 30 minutes. I like to serve this dish on a cold winter night. It's perfect to prepare after work — or for a crowd after skiing or skating. All you need to pass is a big basket of crusty rolls.

Makes 8 servings

¼ pound bacon
1 pound seasoned bulk
   pork sausage
1 pound smoked sausage links,
   sliced
1 can (16 ounces) red kidney
   beans, drained
1 can (16 ounces) white Great
   Northern beans, drained

1 can (16 ounces) stewed
   tomatoes, undrained
2 carrots, thinly sliced
2 ribs celery, sliced
1 clove garlic, minced
1 tablespoon chopped
   fresh parsley
1 teaspoon dried basil

In a Dutch oven, cook bacon over medium heat until crisp. Drain on paper towels. Crumble bacon; set aside.

Discard all but 1 tablespoon bacon drippings. Add bulk sausage and sauté until brown, stirring frequently. Drain well. Add sliced sausage links; sauté briefly. Drain well. Add kidney beans, Great Northern beans, tomatoes with their liquid, carrots, celery, garlic, parsley and basil; mix well. Simmer, covered, 20 minutes. Serve in large soup bowls. Garnish each serving with reserved crumbled bacon.

Sausage and Peppers

Toni Burks
Food Editor, *Roanoke Times & World-News*, Roanoke, VA

I like this recipe because it contains lots of garden-fresh vegetables and it's quick to fix. While the flavors are mingling in the skillet, you can put together a simple green salad and warm some crusty rolls to round out the meal.

Makes 6 to 8 servings

3/4 pound sweet Italian sausage	1 teaspoon dried basil
3/4 pound hot Italian sausage	1 teaspoon dried marjoram
Water	1 teaspoon dried oregano
2 tablespoons olive oil	2 cloves garlic, minced
2 medium onions, cut into wedges	2 cups chopped Italian tomatoes
2 medium green bell peppers,	1/3 cup heavy cream
cut into strips	Hot cooked pasta

Remove casings from sweet and hot sausage; cut sausage into 2-inch chunks. Place sausage in a large skillet with 1/2 inch water. Cook over medium heat until water evaporates. Add olive oil; brown the sausage. Remove sausage from skillet and reserve. Drain excess fat from skillet.

In the same skillet, combine onions, bell peppers, basil, marjoram, oregano and garlic. Cook over medium-high heat until onions begin to brown. Add tomatoes; simmer 5 minutes. Return sausage to skillet; heat 2 minutes. Stir in cream. Heat to serving temperature. Immediately serve sausage mixture over hot cooked pasta.

Note: Sweet (mild) and hot Italian sausage made with poultry can be substituted for Italian sausage made with pork. Use the same amount and prepare in the same way.

Use proper car restraint systems for children.

Sausage-Stuffed Zucchini

Jim Hillibish
City Editor, *The Repository*, Canton, OH

Gardeners know that when the zucchini is ready, only the ready cooks will survive. Otherwise, within just a few days, torpedo-size green vegetables overtake the garden plot. So, it's best to deal with zucchini quickly. Here's a recipe that avoids the usual salad or stir-fry fate of most zukes.

Makes 2 to 4 servings

2 small zucchini
  (4 to 5 inches long)
1/2 pound bulk pork sausage
1 medium green bell pepper,
  chopped
1 small onion, diced

2 cloves garlic, minced
1 teaspoon dried dill weed
Freshly ground black pepper,
  to taste
1 tomato, peeled and chopped
1/4 cup grated Parmesan cheese

Rinse zucchini; pat dry with paper towels. Do not peel. Slice zucchini lengthwise. With a melon baller or spoon, remove zucchini pulp, leaving about 1/4-inch pulp on all sides, to make a shell. Be careful not to make holes in the sides. Save the removed zucchini pulp for salads, breads or other recipes.

In a large skillet, cook sausage until brown, breaking up with a spoon. Drain off fat. Add green pepper, onion, garlic, dill weed and pepper; mix well. Cook until vegetables are tender-crisp.

Stuff each zucchini shell with sausage-vegetable mixture. Put chopped tomato in the bottom of a 9x9x2-inch baking pan or similar shallow pan. Place stuffed zucchini shells on top of tomato, stuffed-side up. Sprinkle with Parmesan cheese. Bake in a preheated 350-degree oven 20 minutes, or until zucchini is tender.

Simple Sauté

Lorrie Guttman
Food Editor, *Tallahassee Democrat*, Tallahassee, FL

How about a recipe with three ingredients? One day I sautéed green cabbage, apples and Polish kielbasa, and discovered what a fortuitous combination that is. The dish, almost a meal in itself, is ready in 10 minutes. I serve apple cider vinegar at the table, to sprinkle atop for added piquancy. In the interest of good nutrition, I go heavy on the cabbage and light on the kielbasa. And I use the lower-fat kielbasa that's readily available in most supermarkets.

Makes 4 servings

1/2 pound lower-fat fully cooked
    Polish kielbasa
1 large head green cabbage

3 medium red apples
Cider vinegar (optional)

Slice sausage 1/4-inch thick. Cook sausage slices in a large skillet over medium-high heat, stirring occasionally, 3 minutes, or until lightly browned. Slice cabbage 1/8-inch thick. Add cabbage to sausage in skillet; stir. Cook, covered, about 5 minutes, or until cabbage is almost tender. Core and slice apples; do not peel. Add apple slices to sausage mixture; stir. Cook, covered, 2 minutes, or until apples are tender. Pass vinegar at the table.

Note: If desired, add 1 tablespoon caraway seeds along with the apples.

Slightly Cajun Pork Chops

Jeanne Voltz
Cookbook Author, Pittsboro, NC

If your cupboard is full of Cajun seasonings given to you by well-meaning friends and family, use some on these chops in place of the seasonings listed here. The lightly spiced chops are the centerpiece of a nourishing meal with freshly cooked green beans or another vegetable, corn on the cob and, for dessert, bread pudding with a fruit sauce.

Makes 4 servings

4 boneless pork chops (1/2-inch thick)	1/4 to 1/2 teaspoon cayenne pepper
1 tablespoon paprika	1 large clove garlic, minced
1/2 teaspoon salt	1 1/2 tablespoons vegetable oil
1 teaspoon dried sage	

Trim any fat from the chops. In a small bowl, combine paprika, salt, sage, pepper and garlic; rub seasoning mixture into the chops.

Heat a large heavy skillet; add oil and heat until almost smoking. Add the chops in a single layer. Reduce heat to medium; sauté chops 8 to 10 minutes, or until browned on both sides, turning three or four times to cook evenly. Place chops on a warm platter and serve immediately.

Soda Pop Chops

Beth Whitley Duke
Food Editor, *Amarillo Globe-News*, Amarillo, TX

Barbecue in Texas is an art form. Every cook has a secret recipe for barbecue sauce. If a cook gives you the old family recipe without a struggle, beware! Savvy cooks have been known to leave out a key ingredient just to keep you guessing. An award-winning restaurateur once told me that the secret of a great barbecue sauce (or marinade, for that matter) is to use something that has an acid content to break down tough meat muscles. His tip gave me the idea to grab a can of Coca-Cola to add to the sauce when I ran out of vinegar one day. Although this recipe uses Coca-Cola for a taste that hails from down Georgia way, you also can experiment with Dr Pepper, a native Texan soft drink invented in Waco and headquartered in Dallas.

Makes 8 servings

8 pork chops
Salt and black pepper, to taste
1 cup ketchup
1 cup carbonated cola beverage
 (such as Coca-Cola or
 Dr Pepper)

¼ cup firmly packed
 brown sugar

Spray a shallow baking dish with non-stick cooking spray. Season chops with salt and pepper, then place pork chops in dish, leaving space between chops for the liquid.

In a small bowl, combine ketchup and carbonated cola beverage; pour over pork chops. Sprinkle brown sugar over chops. Bake, uncovered, in a preheated 350-degree oven 1 hour, or until chops are tender.

Microwave directions: Spray a microwave-safe baking dish with non-stick cooking spray. Place seasoned pork chops in a single layer in dish. (If you must make two layers, try to arrange the chops so that the bone of one is not shielding the one underneath from the microwaves. If the bone deflects the waves, the chops underneath may not cook evenly.) Pour ketchup-cola mixture over chops. Sprinkle brown sugar on top. Cover with plastic wrap, venting one corner. Microwave on High (100 percent) power 5 minutes. Rotate dish ¼ turn. Microwave on Medium (50 percent) power 15 to 20 minutes. Let stand, covered, 3 to 5 minutes to complete cooking.

As many as 1 of every 30 drivers may be legally drunk on a weekend night.

Southern Pork Jumble

Toni Burks
Food Editor, *Roanoke Times & World-News*, Roanoke, VA

Southerners love pork. Why, there's nothin' better on a crisp fall day than a supper of pork roast, sweet potatoes, greens and sautéed apples — unless it's a stir-fried recipe that incorporates all that good stuff.

Makes 4 servings

Seasoning Blend (see recipe)
1 pound boneless pork roast,
   cut into thin strips
1 large sweet potato, peeled and
   cut into thick matchstick pieces
1 red bell pepper, diced
6 green onions, sliced
   (green and white parts)

1 tart green apple, diced
2 tablespoons peanut oil or
   vegetable oil
1/4 cup pecan halves
Steamed greens (kale, turnip,
   mustard, rape, collard or
   a combination)

Prepare Seasoning Blend. Coat pork and sweet potato with 2 tablespoons seasoning blend. Coat bell pepper, green onions and apple with 2 tablespoons seasoning blend.

Heat oil in a large skillet over medium-high heat. Add pork and sweet potato; stir-fry 2 to 3 minutes, or until pork and potato are tender. Add bell pepper, green onions, apple and pecans. Stir-fry 2 minutes. Serve with steamed greens.

Seasoning Blend

3 tablespoons paprika
1/2 teaspoon cayenne pepper
1 tablespoon garlic powder
2 teaspoons dried oregano
2 teaspoons dried thyme

1/2 teaspoon salt
1/2 teaspoon white pepper
1/2 teaspoon ground cumin
1/4 teaspoon ground nutmeg

In a small bowl, combine paprika, cayenne, garlic powder, oregano, thyme, salt, white pepper, cumin and nutmeg. Store in an airtight container in a cool, dry place.

Use as directed to prepare Southern Pork Jumble.

63% of all drivers killed between 9 p.m. and 6 a.m. had a blood alcohol content of .10 or more in 1991.

Sugar and Anise Baked Ham

Susan Manlin Katzman
Free-Lance Food Writer, St. Louis, MO

As far back as I can remember, my father bought delicious hams from a farmer's wife in Alton, Ill. We had these hams at every one of our family's Christmas and Easter celebrations. When the farmer's wife retired, she gave my father a verbal recipe, which he passed along to me. I've made the recipe each Christmas morning for 25 years. I just recently gave the recipe to my daughter, who I hope will treat the family for many years to come. Proportions do not have to be exact, but I suggest using only a bone-in ham because the bone seems to add flavor and substance. Baking time is long enough to heat the ham — prep time is quick and easy.

Makes about 2 large servings per pound

1 whole, fully cooked,
   bone-in ham
About 1/2 teaspoon whole cloves
Cold water

1 to 1 1/2 teaspoons
   anise seeds, divided
Granulated sugar
Paprika

Cut skin and all but a thin layer of fat from ham. Score fat on ham and dot with cloves. Place ham, fat-side up, in a roasting pan. Fill pan with water to a depth of 3/4 inch. Sprinkle 1/2 teaspoon anise seeds over water. Sprinkle about 1 tablespoon sugar and 1/2 teaspoon paprika over ham. Insert a meat thermometer in the thickest part of ham, not touching bone.

Bake in a preheated 325-degree oven until ham reaches an internal temperature of 130 to 135 degrees (approximately 10 minutes per pound). During last half of roasting time, frequently baste ham with pan juices; sprinkle sugar and paprika on ham after each basting. Sprinkle remaining 1/2 to 1 teaspoon anise seeds over ham about 30 minutes before ham is done.

Alcohol involvement is highest in single-vehicle crashes between 9 p.m. - 6 a.m.

Thyme for Pork Chops

Paula M. Galusha
Free-Lance Home Economist, Tulsa, OK

When I was growing up, my mother always cooked pork chops in liquid of some kind for a fairly long time. In the last 10 or so years, pork has changed and so have the methods of cooking it. This is one of my favorites. By varying the herb, you have a different recipe each time.

Makes 4 servings

4 center-cut loin pork chops
    (about 8 ounces each)
Garlic salt

Onion powder
Dried thyme

Place chops on rack of broiler pan; broil 5 inches from heat 5 minutes. Lightly season with garlic salt, onion powder and thyme; broil 3 minutes. Turn chops; broil 5 minutes. Season again with garlic salt, onion powder and thyme; broil 3 minutes, or until cooked through.

Warm Pork and Fruit Salad

Carolyn Flournoy
Food Columnist, *The Times*, Shreveport, LA

In spring, summer or fall, one of my main-dish standbys is a hearty salad. My cousin, a sous chef at a Dallas hotel, gave me her recipe for warm duck salad. Because duck is difficult to come by and expensive, I tried the recipe with pork and think that this version is better than the original.

Makes 4 servings

1/4 cup grapefruit juice
2 tablespoons raspberry vinegar
   or red wine vinegar
1 tablespoon vegetable oil
1 teaspoon poppy seeds
2 teaspoons honey
1 teaspoon Dijon-style mustard
1 pound boneless pork loin,
   thinly sliced

1 head Boston or green
   leaf lettuce
2 pink grapefruit, peeled
   and sectioned
1 1/2 cups seedless green
   grapes, halved
2 or 3 kiwifruit, peeled and sliced

In a jar with a tight-fitting lid, combine grapefruit juice, vinegar, oil, poppy seeds, honey and mustard; shake well. Set dressing aside.

Spray a non-stick skillet with vegetable cooking spray. Heat skillet. Add pork slices and stir-fry 4 to 5 minutes, or just until done.

Line 4 individual serving bowls or plates with equal portions of lettuce leaves; top with equal portions of pork slices, grapefruit sections, halved grapes and kiwifruit slices. Spoon dressing over salads, or pass dressing at the table. Serve immediately.

More than half of all people jailed for drunk driving had previous drunk driving convictions.

Beef

110 Beef and Eggplant Casserole

111 Beef Macaroni Skillet

112 Beef Stroganoff

113 Beefed-Up Kabobs

114 Cabbage Unrolled

115 Campfire Stew

116 Corned Beef and Cabbage for the '90s

116 Different Hamburgers

117 East Meets West Pepper Steak

118 Fabulous Fajitas

119 Filet of Beef with Herb Butter

120 Firehouse Meatballs

121 Great Flank Steak

122 Green Chili Stew

123 Grilled Beef with Mustard Sauce

124 Hamburger and Beans

125 Hamburgers à la Venezia

125 Hungarian Beef Pot

126 Lean Picadillo

127 Mongolian Beef

128 Ogeechee River Goulash

129 Seven League Pizzaburger

130 Spaghetti Nest Pie

131 Spanish Steak

132 Spicy Grilled Steak

133 Steak au Roquefort

134 Taco Casserole

Beef and Eggplant Casserole

Beth W. Orenstein
Staff Writer, *The Express Times*, Easton, PA

This delicious recipe was originally developed for microwave cooking, but it's almost as easy to prepare conventionally as in the microwave oven. Both directions are included here; take your pick. It makes a fast meal that's a good way to use eggplant from the garden.

Makes 4 to 6 servings

1 teaspoon olive oil
1/2 cup chopped onion
1/2 cup chopped green
   bell pepper
1 clove garlic, minced
1 pound lean ground beef
1 medium eggplant, peeled and
   cut into 1/2-inch cubes
   (6 to 8 cups cubes)

1 can (15 ounces) tomato sauce
1/4 teaspoon black pepper
1 cup shredded mozzarella
   cheese (4 ounces)

Heat oil in a large skillet over medium-high heat. Add onion, bell pepper and garlic; cook 3 to 4 minutes, or until vegetables are tender. Add beef; cook until meat is browned, stirring occasionally to break up meat. Drain off fat.

Add cubed eggplant, tomato sauce and pepper to beef and vegetables in skillet; mix well. Transfer to a lightly greased 2-quart baking dish. Bake, covered, in a preheated 350-degree oven 25 minutes. Sprinkle cheese on top. Return to oven and bake 5 minutes, or until cheese melts.

Microwave directions: Put beef in microwave-safe bowl. Microwave on High (100 percent) power 5 to 9 minutes, or until beef loses its pink color, stirring once halfway through cooking time. Drain; set aside.

In a 2-quart round microwave-safe baking dish, combine oil, onion, bell pepper and garlic. Microwave on High 4 to 8 minutes, or until bell pepper is tender. Add cooked beef, cubed eggplant, tomato sauce and pepper to vegetable mixture; mix well. Cover dish with plastic wrap, venting one corner. Microwave on High 12 to 16 minutes, or until eggplant is tender, stirring once or twice during cooking time. Sprinkle cheese on top. Microwave on High 1 to 2 1/2 minutes, or until cheese melts.

Half of the convicted offenders in jail consumed 6 ounces of pure alcohol in 5 hours prior to their arrests for DWI.

Beef Macaroni Skillet

Barbara Mihalevich Arciero
Free-Lance Food Writer, Sacramento, CA

My late stepfather, Joe Goodnight of Shelbina, Mo., was known far and wide for being as stubborn as a Missouri mule when it came to trying new foods. He was a meat-and-potatoes man who was suspicious of anything mixed, like a casserole or skillet supper. Determined to break their routine of fried chicken, roast beef, country-cured ham, T-bone steaks and other on-the-farm entrées, my mother clipped this recipe from the Hannibal Courier-Post and crossed her fingers. He loved it.

Makes 6 servings

1 pound lean ground beef	1 tablespoon cider vinegar
1 medium onion, chopped	1 teaspoon dry mustard
3 cups tomato juice	1 teaspoon salt
1 cup uncooked elbow macaroni	1/8 teaspoon black pepper
1 tablespoon Worcestershire sauce	

In a large skillet, brown beef with onion; drain off fat. Add tomato juice, macaroni, Worcestershire sauce, vinegar, dry mustard, salt and pepper; mix well. Bring to a boil. Reduce heat; simmer, covered, 20 minutes, or until macaroni is tender. Stir occasionally during cooking.

Note: One pound ground turkey can be substituted for the ground beef.

Beef Stroganoff

Louise Bentley
Food Editor, *Chippewa Herald Telegram*, Chippewa Falls, WI

One day, while looking through my recipes for something different to make, I found two hand-written recipes for Beef Stroganoff. There were some ingredients that I liked in each of the recipes, so I decided to use some items from both recipes. The result was the following hybrid recipe, which proved to be a hit with my husband and two daughters. I wrote my version on a different card and use it when I am looking for something easy yet special for my family.

Makes 5 to 6 servings

1/4 cup butter or margarine
2 to 2 1/2 pounds boneless beef round steak, cut into cubes
Dash salt
Dash black pepper
1 can (10 3/4 ounces) condensed cream of tomato soup, undiluted
1 can (10 1/2 ounces) beef consommé, divided
1 small onion, sliced
1 can (4 ounces) sliced mushrooms, drained
1/4 cup all-purpose flour
3 cups cooked egg noodles

Melt butter in a large skillet; add steak cubes and brown all over. Add salt, pepper, tomato soup and half of the beef consommé. Stir to make a smooth sauce. Add onion and mushrooms. Cover and simmer 1 hour, stirring occasionally.

In a small bowl, combine flour and the remaining half of the beef consommé. Stir until smooth. Slowly stir flour mixture into steak mixture. Cook over medium-high heat, stirring constantly, until mixture is thickened. Serve over noodles.

Experts estimate that direct costs of drunk driving, cost the United States $46 billion each year.

Beefed-Up Kabobs

Sally Cappon
Food Columnist, *Santa Barbara News-Press*, Santa Barbara, CA

For years, our family has used this basic marinade recipe, which I originally got from a friend in Wisconsin. Over the years, the ingredients have evolved. Although this recipe calls for top sirloin, the marinade is also delicious with shrimp and seafood; try it with thresher shark for a real treat. These kabobs receive raves everytime I serve them — and they're fast and easy, too.

Makes 4 servings

1/3 cup red wine vinegar
1/4 cup ketchup
2 tablespoons olive oil
2 tablespoons soy sauce
1 tablespoon Worcestershire sauce
1 teaspoon Dijon-style mustard
1 teaspoon salt
1/4 teaspoon freshly ground black pepper
2 cloves garlic, minced
1 pound beef top sirloin, cut into 3/4-inch cubes
Cherry tomatoes, mushrooms, small onions, green bell pepper chunks (optional)

In a small bowl, combine vinegar, ketchup, olive oil, soy sauce, Worcestershire sauce, mustard, salt, pepper and garlic; mix well. Place beef cubes in a shallow non-metallic container; pour marinade over meat. Marinate, covered, in refrigerator 2 hours or longer, turning meat occasionally.

Remove meat from marinade, reserving marinade. Thread meat onto skewers, alternating beef cubes with tomatoes, mushrooms, onions and bell peppers, as desired. Meanwhile, heat reserved marinade to boiling, then simmer 5 minutes.

Grill kabobs over hot coals 10 to 15 minutes, or until meat is done, turning kabobs frequently and basting meat with warmed marinade. Discard any remaining marinade.

Cabbage Unrolled

Patricia G. Gray
News Assistant, *The Express-Times*, Easton, PA

Known by many names and using bread, bread crumbs or rice as a meat stretcher, stuffed cabbage is part of the culinary heritage of many ethnic groups. Our family called the dish cabbage rolls when I was growing up, which is why my recipe is called Cabbage Unrolled. Instead of steaming the cabbage leaves and rolling the meat mixture in them, I save time by simply chopping the cabbage and layering it with the meatballs. The dish cooks more quickly and it also eliminates the problem of how to keep the cabbage leaves from unrolling during cooking.

Makes 4 to 6 servings

1 small head cabbage
   (about 1 pound),
   coarsely chopped
1 pound lean ground beef
1/2 cup instant rice, uncooked

1 small onion, finely chopped
1/2 teaspoon salt (optional)
1/8 teaspoon black pepper
1 can (15 ounces) tomato purée
1 can (14 1/2 ounces) beef broth

Place one-third of the cabbage in the bottom of a large, deep skillet or Dutch oven. In a bowl, combine beef, rice, onion, salt and pepper. Form into meatballs. Place half of the meatballs on top of the cabbage. Cover with one-third of the cabbage and the rest of the meatballs. Top with the remaining one-third of the cabbage. Pour tomato purée and beef broth over all. Bring to a boil. Reduce heat and simmer, covered, 20 minutes, or until meat is cooked through.

More people are arrested for drunk driving each year than any other crime.

Campfire Stew

Lorrie Guttman
Food Editor, *Tallahassee Democrat*, Tallahassee, FL

We recently did a story about campfire cooking, and I found myself using some of the recipes at home. This one couldn't be easier, and my family loves it. The basic recipe called for just ground beef and alphabet soup, with the option of adding potatoes and carrots. I had fresh spinach on hand and added it to the stew, with great results. To dress it up even more, I added Italian herbs and topped the stew with freshly grated Parmesan cheese.

Makes 4 servings

1 large potato, cubed
1 large carrot, sliced
2 1/2 cups water
1/2 pound extra-lean ground beef
2 cans (10 3/4 ounces each)
    condensed alphabet soup,
    undiluted

3 cups firmly packed, chopped
    fresh spinach
1 teaspoon Italian herbs
Freshly grated Parmesan cheese

In a large saucepan, boil potato and carrot in water until vegetables are almost cooked through. Meanwhile, brown ground beef in a medium skillet; drain fat. Add beef to potato, carrot and water in saucepan. Add alphabet soup, spinach and Italian herbs. Mix well; simmer about 3 minutes. Sprinkle Parmesan cheese over each serving.

Note: If you don't want to use the potato and carrot, you can simply brown the ground beef in a pot, then add 2 soup cans of water along with the other ingredients. Cook as directed.

Corned Beef and Cabbage for the '90s

Carolyn Flournoy
Food Columnist, *The Times*, Shreveport, LA

> *Like the cartoon character Jiggs, my husband's favorite dish is corned beef and cabbage. Now that corned beef is available at most delis and supermarkets, I make what I call Corned Beef and Cabbage for the '90s.*

Makes 3 to 4 servings

1 small head cabbage
2 cups water
1 teaspoon lemon juice
1/2 teaspoon salt
1/2 teaspoon granulated sugar

1/4 teaspoon garlic powder
Caraway seeds, to taste (optional)
1/2 pound corned beef
   (from a deli or supermarket)

Rinse cabbage; core and cut into small wedges. In a large stockpot or Dutch oven, combine cabbage, water, lemon juice, salt, sugar, garlic powder and caraway seeds. (The caraway seeds help cut the odor of cooking cabbage. They also help cut the odor of boiling shrimp.) Bring mixture to a boil; cover and simmer 8 to 10 minutes. Add corned beef, whole or in slices, whichever you prefer. Cook, covered, 5 to 6 minutes.

Note: For an old-fashioned boiled dinner, add 2 sliced carrots and 1 cubed potato to the cabbage mixture.

Different Hamburgers

Stacy Lam
Reporter, *The Macon Telegraph*, Macon, GA

> *This recipe adds a little pizzazz to a cook-out classic. I've made these burgers many times for guests, and they've always been a hit, even with kids. I think they're best served on big, fresh onion rolls.*

Makes 14 servings

3 pounds lean ground beef
1 1/3 cups crushed corn flakes
1 cup dairy sour cream
1/4 cup soy sauce

3 teaspoons dried minced onion
1/2 teaspoon lemon-pepper
   seasoning salt

Only 1 out of every 2,000 drunk drivers is ever arrested.

In a large mixing bowl, combine beef, corn flakes, sour cream, soy sauce, onion and lemon-pepper seasoning salt; mix well. Shape meat mixture into 14 patties. Grill over medium-hot coals 8 minutes per side, or until done to taste.

East Meets West Pepper Steak

Beth Whitley Duke
Food Editor, *Amarillo Globe-News*, Amarillo, TX

Amarillo is a town of about 175,000 people in the middle of the panhandle of Texas. Visitors expect to find great Texas steaks, ranch-style barbecue and red-hot Tex-Mex cooking along the Texas stretch of Interstates 40 and 27. But Amarillo restaurants offer other treasures as well, thanks to the influence of newer Texans from Indochina and Asia. Cafés with names such as the Thai Star, My Thai, Peking and Hunan have taught Texans that jalapeños are not the only way to turn up the temperature for your taste buds.

Makes 6 servings

3 tablespoons butter or
   vegetable oil
1 1/2 pounds beef round or flank
   steak, cut into 1/4-wide strips
1 1/2 cups thinly sliced onions
1 cup diced celery
2 cups chopped tomatoes
1 1/2 teaspoons salt
1/2 teaspoon black pepper

1 teaspoon granulated sugar
2 bay leaves
1/2 teaspoon dried thyme
3 large green bell peppers,
   cut into thin strips
1 1/2 teaspoons cornstarch
2 teaspoons soy sauce
1/4 cup cold water
Hot cooked rice

Heat butter or oil in heavy skillet or wok over high heat. Add meat in 2 or 3 batches, so that each batch just covers the bottom of skillet without crowding; brown meat. Remove browned meat from skillet and set aside.

Reduce heat. Add onions; sauté 5 minutes. Return meat to skillet. Add celery, tomatoes, salt, pepper, sugar, bay leaves and thyme. Simmer 30 minutes. Add bell peppers; simmer 10 minutes.

In a small bowl, blend cornstarch, soy sauce and water. Stir into meat mixture. Cook 1 minute, or until sauce is thick and clear. Serve over hot rice.

Fabulous Fajitas

Beth Whitley Duke
Food Editor, *Amarillo Globe-News*, Amarillo, TX

Fajitas is a Spanish word that means, literally, little belts or sashes. The word refers to the thin strips of beef called skirt steaks that a butcher cuts from legs of beef. This economical cut of meat is too tough to eat without first marinating it in lime juice to break down the muscle tissue. The word also refers to a popular dish made with this cut of meat. Fajitas are a south Texas tradition that has slowly migrated northward from the Texas-Mexico border. With the growing influence of Southwest cuisine, fajitas appear on menus all across the country with almost endless variations on the theme. They're easy to prepare at home, too. One word of warning: Spanish-speaking people almost always chuckle when someone orders chicken fajitas because the term conjures up a funny word picture of a chicken with tiny sashes on its legs.

Makes 4 servings

2 pounds beef skirt steak
(flank steak is a good
substitute)
1/2 cup fresh lime juice
1/4 cup olive oil
3 to 4 cloves garlic, minced
1 teaspoon salt
1/2 teaspoon black pepper

Condiments such as dairy sour
cream, grated cheese,
chopped lettuce, chopped
tomatoes, picante sauce,
sliced avocados and/or
chopped onion, as desired
8 (8-inch) flour tortillas

Cut membrane from skirt steak, or, if using flank steak, cut meat into strips. Put meat in a shallow non-metallic container. In a small bowl, combine lime juice, oil, garlic, salt and pepper; pour marinade over meat. Marinate, covered, in the refrigerator at least 30 minutes (4 to 6 hours is better, if you have the time).

While the meat marinates, prepare the condiments. For 4 servings, you will need about 3/4 cup of each topping. Stack the tortillas and wrap tightly in foil. Heat tortillas in a preheated 350-degree oven 15 minutes.

Drain meat, discarding marinade. Grill meat 4 to 5 minutes per side, or until done to taste. Traditionalists use an outdoor grill, but a heavy stovetop griddle or cast-iron skillet works well, too.

A .02 blood alcohol content can impair driving abilities and increase the chances of a crash.

To serve, let guests assemble their own fajitas by placing a portion of meat in the middle of a warm tortilla and topping it with their choice of condiments.

Note: For chicken fajitas, use 2 pounds skinned, boned chicken breasts. Marinate as directed. Drain, then grill 8 to 10 minutes per side, or until done to taste. Slice cooked chicken into strips. Assemble fajitas as directed.

Filet of Beef with Herb Butter

Lori Longbotham
Free-Lance Food Writer, Astoria, NY

You'll have this steak with its own delicious "sauce" on the table in no time. Even though it is beef and butter, it is still within the latest guidelines for healthful eating — so you don't have to give up a good steak to stay healthy. Enjoy it and remember it's high in vitamin B-12 and zinc.

Makes 2 servings

1 tablespoon unsalted butter,
   at room temperature
1 small shallot, minced
1/2 teaspoon minced fresh chives
1/2 teaspoon minced
   fresh parsley
1/4 teaspoon minced
   fresh tarragon, plus
   sprigs for garnish

Pinch grated lemon peel
Pinch salt
Pinch freshly ground black pepper
2 beef filet mignons
   (3 ounces each),
   completely trimmed

In a small bowl, combine butter, shallot, chives, parsley, minced tarragon, lemon peel, salt and pepper; mix well. Shape into a 1-inch long cylinder; wrap in plastic wrap. Freeze at least 1 hour, or until firm. (If desired, butter mixture can be used at room temperature without freezing.)

Put filets on broiler pan. Broil in a preheated broiler 4 to 5 inches from heat 4 minutes on each side for medium-rare, or until done to taste.

Cut butter mixture crosswise into 6 slices. Top each hot filet with 3 butter slices. Garnish with tarragon sprigs. Serve immediately.

Firehouse Meatballs

Suzanne Hall
Food Editor, *The Chattanooga Times*, Chattanooga, TN

Who says kids don't cook? They do in Chattanooga. This easy recipe was developed for a class assignment by a fifth-grade student in a local school. (I'll bet you can guess what his father does for a living!) You can serve these meatballs as the main course with a green vegetable and potatoes or add them to your favorite tomato sauce and serve with spaghetti.

Makes 4 to 6 servings

1 pound lean ground beef
1/2 cup corn flakes, crushed
1/2 cup evaporated milk
1/4 cup finely chopped onions
1/4 cup chili sauce
1 tablespoon Worcestershire
  sauce

1 teaspoon salt
1/4 teaspoon black pepper
1 teaspoon hot pepper sauce
  (optional)

In a 2-quart bowl, combine ground beef, corn flakes, evaporated milk, onions, chili sauce, Worcestershire sauce, salt, pepper and hot pepper sauce; mix well. With wet hands, shape mixture into 16 meatballs. Place meatballs in an ungreased 13x9x2-inch baking pan. Bake, uncovered, in a preheated 400-degree oven 20 minutes, or until lightly browned on the outside and cooked medium on the inside.

At .08 blood alcohol content, your risk of being in a crash is 3 to 4 times more than when sober.

Great Flank Steak

Susan Manlin Katzman
Free-Lance Food Writer, St. Louis, MO

When I submitted the copy for my first cookbook to a publisher, I was told that I should omit the lemonade recipe because it was "just too easy to make." "Nonsense," I replied, "there is no such thing as too easy when it comes to good food." The lemonade recipe remained. Here is another of those recipes that some might consider just too easy, but that I consider just right. I have tried many flank steak recipes and this remains far better than the rest. Although made from just two ingredients, the marinade gives the steak a wonderful browned exterior and intensifies the flavor of the beef itself rather than masking it with additional flavors. The steak is great served thinly sliced, straight from the grill. It is also terrific served cold in sandwiches or salads.

Makes 4 to 5 servings

1 beef flank steak
(about 2 pounds)
About 1/3 cup soy sauce

About 1/3 cup Worcestershire
sauce

Score flank steak with a sharp knife; put steak in a shallow non-metallic container. Combine soy sauce and Worcestershire sauce; pour over steak. Marinate steak 2 to 4 hours, turning steak occasionally to evenly coat steak with marinade. (To eliminate the need for turning, cover steak with equal amounts of soy sauce and Worcestershire sauce.)

Remove steak from marinade; discard marinade. Either broil steak under high heat or grill over moderately hot coals 4 to 5 minutes, or until steak is browned on one side. Turn steak over with tongs and brown other side. Do not overcook. This steak should be served rare. Let steak rest 10 minutes before slicing. Slice across the grain, diagonally, into thin strips.

Green Chili Stew

Mary Beth Jung
Free-Lance Food Writer, Grafton, WI

Green Chili Stew is a favorite regional dish of the Southwest. I first tasted it while visiting a friend in New Mexico. She served this hearty, well-seasoned stew with a guacamole salad and warm flour tortillas. Don't be afraid of the chilies; they are quite mild. This is a perfect dish to prepare ahead of time and reheat for a winter after-ski or skating party.

Makes about 6 servings

2 pounds beef round steak,
    cut into 1 1/2-inch cubes
1/4 cup all-purpose flour
Salt and black pepper, to taste
2 tablespoons vegetable oil
2 large onions, chopped
2 cans (4 ounces each) chopped
    green chilies, drained

1 can (14 1/2 ounces)
    tomatoes, undrained
1 cup water
1 garlic clove, minced
Warm flour tortillas

Dredge steak cubes in flour seasoned with salt and pepper. Heat oil in a Dutch oven. Add steak cubes and onions; cook until meat is brown and onions are tender. Add chilies, tomatoes with their liquid, water, garlic and salt to taste. Mix well, breaking up tomatoes with the back of a spoon. Simmer, covered, about 1 hour, or until meat is tender. Taste and adjust seasonings. Serve stew with tortillas.

You have about a 40% chance of being in an alcohol-related crash during your lifetime.

Grilled Beef with Mustard Sauce

Jeanne Voltz
Cookbook Author, Pittsboro, NC

*This recipe is reminiscent of old-fashioned steak house presentations —
crusty-brown beef with a rich sauce. But looks are deceiving. Use a lean
cut of beef, such as top round, and trim it well. The sauce can be made
with either yogurt or sour cream. Oven-roasted or steamed new potatoes
with fresh thyme or dill make a favorite, and easy, meal with the steak.*

Makes 4 to 5 servings

2 tablespoons Dijon-style mustard
2 tablespoons balsamic vinegar
   or red wine vinegar
1/4 teaspoon freshly ground
   black pepper
4 tablespoons olive oil, divided

2 green onions, sliced very thin
   (green and white parts)
1/2 cup plain yogurt or dairy
   sour cream
1 1/2 pounds beef top round
   steak (about 1-inch thick)

In a small bowl, whisk together mustard, vinegar and pepper. Gradually
whisk in 3 tablespoons oil; blend until smooth. Stir in green onions and
yogurt. Set sauce aside.

Preheat a heavy skillet or charcoal, electric or gas grill until hot. Wipe
the meat with paper towels, then brush both sides with the remaining 1
tablespoon olive oil. Grill steak over high heat until well browned on one
side; turn and brown the other side. Allow 10 minutes cooking time for
medium-rare. Cut a slit near the center with a small knife; if done to taste,
remove from heat. If not, reduce heat and cook 1 to 2 minutes, or until done
to taste. (This cut of beef is best if cooked no more than medium-rare.)

Place cooked beef on a board or platter; carve across the grain into
1/2-inch slices. Place a spoonful of sauce on each serving and pass the
remaining sauce at the table.

Hamburger and Beans

Christine Randall
Assistant Features Editor, *The Post and Courier*, Charleston, SC

My mother has prepared this recipe for years, and it has always been one of my favorites. It's easy to make, doesn't require any exotic ingredients, and if you're not in the mood for hamburger, you can substitute hot dogs instead. It's kind of soupy, so you really could serve it in a bowl like chili.

Makes 4 to 6 servings

4 slices bacon	1/2 cup molasses
1 pound lean ground beef	1/2 cup ketchup
1 onion, chopped	2 teaspoons Worcestershire sauce
2 cans (16 ounces each)	1 teaspoon salt, or to taste
pork and beans	1/2 teaspoon dry mustard

In a large skillet, cook bacon until crisp. Transfer to paper towels to drain. Crumble bacon; reserve.

Drain fat from skillet. In same skillet, cook beef and onion until meat is brown. Pour off excess fat. Add pork and beans, molasses, ketchup, Worcestershire sauce, salt and dry mustard to beef and onion in skillet; mix well.

Transfer mixture to an ungreased 2-quart baking dish. Top with reserved crumbled bacon. Bake in a preheated 350-degree oven 20 to 30 minutes.

Hamburgers à la Venezia

Constance Hay
Free-Lance Food Writer, Columbia, MD

On those nights when you are too tired to cook anything except hamburgers, go ahead and make them, but give them a new taste with herbs. Just close your eyes and pretend you are in Italy.

Makes 4 to 6 servings

1 pound lean ground beef	2 teaspoons Italian seasoning
1 onion, finely chopped	1 teaspoon salt
1/3 cup chopped fresh parsley	1/4 teaspoon black pepper

In a medium mixing bowl, combine beef, onion, parsley, Italian seasoning, salt and pepper; mix well. Form into patties. Broil, grill or fry until done to taste.

Hungarian Beef Pot

Carolyn Flournoy
Food Columnist, *The Times*, Shreveport, LA

My mother studied to be an opera singer but ended up being a part-time accountant, homemaker and excellent cook. Her Hungarian voice teacher gave her this recipe which can be prepared in less than 30 minutes and is an excellent dish for company. I like to serve it with a spinach salad. P.S. I can't even carry a tune.

Makes 4 servings

1 pound lean ground beef	1 cup dairy sour cream
1 medium onion, chopped	1 to 2 teaspoons sweet
1/2 cup beef broth	Hungarian paprika
2 tablespoons tomato paste	1 package (16 ounces)
1 teaspoon prepared mustard	egg noodles,
1/4 teaspoon garlic powder	cooked and drained

In a heavy skillet, brown meat. Stir in onion; cook until soft. Stir in beef broth, tomato paste, mustard and garlic powder. Simmer, covered, 6 to 8 minutes. Stir in sour cream and paprika; heat slowly to prevent sour cream from curdling. Do not allow mixture to boil. Serve beef mixture over hot cooked noodles.

Approximately 28,000 people were killed in alcohol-related crashes in 1980.

Lean Picadillo

Mary D. Scourtes
Food Writer, *The Tampa Tribune*, Tampa, FL

Picadillo is an old Tampa favorite that you'll find in every Spanish restaurant in town. Originally made with almost a cup of oil, this version is scaled down for the lean, mean '90s cook who thinks of speed and nutrition.

Makes 6 servings

2 teaspoons olive oil
1 large onion, chopped
1 medium green bell pepper
1 clove garlic, minced
1 pound lean ground beef
1 can (15 ounces) tomato sauce
1/2 cup chopped pitted
   black olives

2 to 4 tablespoons capers, to taste
1 teaspoon Worcestershire sauce
1/2 teaspoon dried oregano
1/4 teaspoon ground cinnamon
Hot pepper sauce, to taste
   (optional)
Hot cooked rice or toasted
   hamburger buns

Heat oil in a large skillet over medium-high heat. Add onion, bell pepper and garlic; sauté 2 to 3 minutes. Add beef; cook until meat is browned on all sides. Drain off fat. Add tomato sauce, olives, capers, Worcestershire sauce, oregano and cinnamon; mix well. Cook 15 minutes to blend flavors. Season to taste with hot pepper sauce. Serve over hot rice or toasted hamburger buns.

 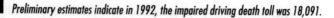 *Preliminary estimates indicate in 1992, the impaired driving death toll was 18,091.*

Mongolian Beef

Mary Beth Jung
Free-Lance Food Writer, Grafton, WI

This dish is especially pretty because of the matchstick shapes of the ingredients. I buy the bamboo shoots at an Asian grocery because they sell them already cut into matchsticks. While you're at the Asian grocery, stock up on chili paste with garlic, hoisin sauce and a good-quality soy sauce. I use the dark variety of soy sauce, which gives this dish a rich flavor and color.

Makes 4 servings

1 pound broccoli (without stems), cut into small florets
1/3 cup chicken broth
1/4 cup hoisin sauce
1/4 cup dark soy sauce
2 tablespoons cornstarch
1/2 to 1 teaspoon chili paste with garlic
2 tablespoons peanut oil
1 pound beef flank steak, cut into matchsticks (julienned)
1/3 cup matchstick (julienned) bamboo shoots
6 green onions, thinly sliced (green and white parts)
Hot cooked rice

In a large saucepan or steamer, steam broccoli until tender-crisp. Set aside.

In a small bowl, combine chicken broth, hoisin sauce, soy sauce, cornstarch and chili paste; mix well. Set sauce aside.

Heat a wok or large skillet over high heat. Add oil and heat. Add steak to hot oil; stir-fry until meat is just pink. Add bamboo shoots and green onions. Stir-fry 1 minute.

Stir the reserved sauce; add to mixture in wok. Cook and stir until thickened. Transfer meat mixture to serving platter. Garnish with a ring of reserved steamed broccoli. Serve immediately, with hot rice.

Ogeechee River Goulash

Louise Dodd
Food Editor, *Courier Herald*, Dublin, GA

*My family often retreated to our primitive cabin in the swamps of
Georgia's dark-water Ogeechee River when my father closed his store for
holidays. Although Mother's little cooking stove was fueled by a tank of
kerosene hanging on the side that emitted ferocious fumes, it in no way
diminished the good cooking that dominated our trips. I still remember
when Mother and Aunt Maude introduced this delicious dish to us on the
4th of July, 1936. It is indeed a memorable dish.*

Makes 6 servings

2 pounds lean ground beef
1 teaspoon salt
1/2 teaspoon black pepper
1 cup chopped onions
1/2 cup chopped celery
1/4 cup chopped green
    bell pepper

1 teaspoon paprika
1 teaspoon Worcestershire sauce
2 cans (16 ounces each)
    tomatoes, undrained
Hot cooked rice

In a large skillet, brown beef; pour off grease. Remove beef from skillet;
season beef with salt and pepper.

In the same skillet, sauté onions, celery and bell pepper until tender.
Return cooked beef to skillet. Add paprika and Worcestershire sauce; mix
well. Add tomatoes, which have been pulverized with a blender or mashed
with a fork. Cook over low heat about 30 minutes to blend flavors. Serve
over rice.

About 50 people are killed each day in alcohol-related crashes.

Seven League Pizzaburger

Sally Cappon
Food Columnist, *Santa Barbara News-Press*, Santa Barbara, CA

I've had this recipe forever. The recipe card has been handled so much that it's practically illegible, wearing the patina of gold that is the measure of a true treasure. This is my kids' favorite supper—a sure-fire winner when I'm out of ideas and time.

Makes 5 to 6 servings

1 pound extra-lean ground beef
1 can (10 3/4 ounces) condensed cream of tomato soup, undiluted
1/2 cup chopped onion
1/3 cup grated Parmesan cheese
1/3 cup ketchup
1/4 cup chopped green or red bell pepper
1 teaspoon dried oregano
1/2 teaspoon salt
1/4 teaspoon garlic salt
1 loaf French bread, cut in half lengthwise
1 cup grated sharp Cheddar cheese

In a large skillet, brown ground beef. Drain fat. Add tomato soup, onion, Parmesan cheese, ketchup, bell pepper, oregano, salt and garlic salt; mix well. Bring to a boil. Reduce heat; simmer 3 to 5 minutes to blend flavors.

Spread meat mixture on cut sides of bread. Sprinkle cheese on meat mixture. Put "pizzas" under broiler until cheese is bubbly and golden. Cut into diagonal slices to serve.

Spaghetti Nest Pie

Jim Hillibish
City Editor, *The Repository*, Canton, OH

Quick main courses need not be bland to the eyes or the taste buds. This recipe is fun to prepare as well as to eat. When people see it come out of the oven, they wonder just what in the world is this pie.

Makes 4 to 6 servings

1 package (8 ounces) uncooked thin spaghetti
2 tablespoons butter or margarine
1/2 cup grated Parmesan or Romano cheese
2 eggs, beaten
1 1/2 cups cottage cheese
1 pound lean ground beef
1/2 cup chopped onion
1 clove garlic
1/4 cup chopped green bell pepper
1 can (8 ounces) tomatoes, undrained, coarsely chopped
1 can (6 ounces) tomato paste
1 teaspoon granulated sugar
3 teaspoons dried oregano
1 cup shredded mozzarella cheese

Cook spaghetti according to package directions; drain thoroughly. While spaghetti is still hot, stir in butter, Parmesan cheese and eggs. Let mixture cool 3 to 4 minutes while you grease a 10-inch pie plate. Form spaghetti mixture into a "crust" in the plate. Spread cottage cheese inside the spaghetti crust.

In a large skillet, cook beef with onion, garlic and bell pepper. Pour off fat. Add tomatoes with their liquid, tomato paste, sugar and oregano to meat mixture; mix well. Cook 3 to 4 minutes.

Spoon meat mixture over cottage cheese in the spaghetti crust. Bake, uncovered, in a preheated 350-degree oven 25 minutes. Sprinkle mozzarella cheese on top. Return to oven and bake 5 minutes, or until cheese melts.

Note: Any leftovers can be refrigerated for up to 4 days. The baked pie also can be frozen. Reheat in a microwave oven.

About 318,000 people were injured in alcohol-related crashes in 1991.

Spanish Steak

Sue Kurth
Food Editor, *Beloit Daily News*, Beloit, WI

This recipe is one my mother passed on to me when I married. It has always been a favorite, but became even more so after I began working outside the home. This dish can be whipped up in a hurry and popped into the oven. While it bakes, you can set the table and prepare the remainder of the meal. Because the sauce is zesty, I like to serve this dish with mild-flavored accompaniments, such as mashed potatoes and green beans. The sauce from the steak makes a great gravy for the potatoes.

Makes 6 servings

1 ½ pounds beef round steak
    (about ½-inch thick)
¾ teaspoon salt
Dash black pepper
1 medium onion, sliced
½ green bell pepper, chopped
1 can (4 ounces) mushroom
    pieces, drained

2 cans (8 ounces each)
    tomato sauce
2 tablespoons lemon juice
1 bay leaf
3 or 4 whole cloves

Cut beef into serving-size pieces. Put pieces in a lightly greased 2-quart baking dish. Season with salt and pepper. Scatter onion, bell pepper and mushrooms over meat.

In a medium saucepan, combine tomato sauce, lemon juice, bay leaf and cloves; bring to a simmer over medium heat. Pour sauce over meat and vegetables in baking dish. Bake, covered, in a preheated 350-degree oven 1 ½ hours, or until meat is tender.

Spicy Grilled Steak

Leona Carlson
Food Writer (Retired), *Rockford Register Star*, Rockford, IL

This easy and economical entrée was much in demand at our house when my children were teenagers. Now they're serving it to their own children, and I'm still getting compliments from my guests. Best of all, leftovers can be refrigerated, sliced thin and used for sandwiches, or microwaved briefly and served as a hot entrée for a quick pick-up dinner the second time around.

Makes 4 servings

1 envelope (1 1/2 ounces)
   spaghetti sauce mix
1/4 cup vegetable oil

1/4 cup lemon juice
1/4 cup ketchup
1 beef flank steak (about 1 pound)

In a small bowl, combine spaghetti sauce mix, oil, lemon juice and ketchup; mix well. Put steak in shallow non-metallic container. Pour marinade over steak. Refrigerate, covered, 30 minutes to 1 hour, turning once. Drain meat, reserving marinade.

Heat marinade in small saucepan to boiling; simmer 5 minutes. Keep warm, for use as basting sauce.

Broil steak in oven broiler or grill over hot coals 5 to 10 minutes on each side (depending on broiler or grill and thickness of steak), or until done to taste; baste occasionally with warmed marinade.

When meat is cooked as desired, carve crosswise into thin slices. Discard any remaining marinade.

About 27 fewer people die in alcohol-related crashes every day since MADD began in 1980.

Steak au Roquefort

Paula M. Galusha
Free-Lance Home Economist, Tulsa, OK

An elegant steak dinner is always a pleasure, but doing something a little different to steak can be a challenge. This recipe is one I keep close at hand — actually, I've memorized it — for dinners that can be prepared quickly and really make a statement. Served with baked potatoes, peas and a tossed salad, the steak is a favorite with almost everyone.

Makes 4 servings

6 ounces Roquefort cheese,
  crumbled
2 tablespoons cream cheese,
  softened
2 tablespoons milk
1 tablespoon chopped fresh chives

1 teaspoon Worcestershire sauce
Freshly ground black pepper
Salt
4 boneless beef rib steaks
  (about 8 ounces each)

In a small bowl, combine Roquefort cheese, cream cheese, milk, chives, Worcestershire sauce and pepper; mix well. Set aside.

Sprinkle a light layer of salt over the bottom of a large skillet; place skillet over medium-high heat. When salt is hot, add steaks to skillet. Cook steaks to desired doneness. Transfer steaks to warm platter and keep warm.

Pour reserved cheese mixture into skillet; heat. Serve hot cheese mixture over steaks.

Taco Casserole

Dorothy Cunningham
Free-Lance Writer, Morenci, MI

Each summer, hundreds of Hispanic workers arrive in our area to help with the harvest of cherries, apples, tomatoes and other vegetables. Many do not return to their homes in Mexico in the fall, but settle down to add their ethnic flavor to our community. As a result, we have a great many small Mexican restaurants in the area. This recipe for Taco Casserole, while not strictly a Mexican dish, is a local favorite that's quick-to-fix. A version of it was included in a cookbook published by the Adrian United Methodist Church.

Makes 6 servings

1 pound lean ground beef
1 envelope (1 1/2 ounces) taco
   seasoning mix
1 can (16 ounces) refried beans
2 cups water
1 package (8 ounces) taco-flavor
   tortilla chips, crumbled

2 cups grated Cheddar cheese
   (about 8 ounces)
Chopped lettuce
Chopped tomatoes
Salsa (homemade or commercial)
Dairy sour cream or plain
   low-fat yogurt

In a large skillet, brown ground beef; drain off fat. Add taco seasoning mix, refried beans and water. Heat mixture, stirring occasionally, until it begins to boil.

Spread tortilla chips in the bottom of a 9x9x2-inch baking dish. Pour meat mixture over chips. Sprinkle cheese on top. Bake in a preheated 350-degree oven 15 to 20 minutes, or until cheese begins to bubble.

Pass lettuce, tomatoes, salsa and sour cream at the table and let each diner add toppings of choice to his/her serving.

Even one drunk driving death is too many.

Lamb, Game & Other Meats

136 Braised Lamb Shanks

137 Chicken Liver Risotto

138 Creole Hot Dogs

139 Curried Rack of Lamb

140 Curry in a Hurry

140 Ginger Chops

141 Greek-Style Lamb Kabobs

142 Lamb Chops with
     Orange-Apricot Couscous

143 Lamb Shanks with
     Potatoes and Blue Cheese

144 Medallions of Venison with
     Blueberries

145 Moussaka with
     Zucchini or Eggplant

146 Oriental Liver

147 Roasted Leg of Lamb

148 Ruby Lamb

149 Spicy Lamb and Lentil Stew

150 Veal with Chanterelles

151 Venison Pepper Steak

152 Venison Roast, German Style

153 Venison Salad

Braised Lamb Shanks

Doris Reynolds
Food Columnist, *Naples Daily News*, Naples, FL

Lamb shanks are inexpensive, delicious and easy to prepare. This recipe comes from The Golden Lamb, a historic restaurant/inn in Lebanon, Ohio, a short distance from Cincinnati. This dish is especially good with wild rice, polenta or barley. Although the dish bakes for 2 hours, the actual preparation time is short and you can do other things while it is baking.

Makes 4 to 6 servings

4 to 6 lamb shanks
  (about 4 to 6 pounds total)
1 teaspoon salt
1/4 teaspoon black pepper
3 tablespoons olive oil or
  vegetable oil
1 cup diced onions
1 cup sliced fresh mushrooms
  (about 1/4 pound)
1 cup diced turnips

3/4 cup diced celery
1/3 cup all-purpose flour
3 tablespoons tomato paste
1/4 teaspoon fresh rosemary
  (or 1/8 teaspoon dried)
1/4 teaspoon fresh thyme
  (or 1/8 teaspoon dried)
1 large bay leaf
2 cloves garlic, minced
3 1/2 cups lamb or beef stock

Season lamb shanks with salt and pepper. Heat oil in large Dutch oven or heavy roaster. Brown lamb shanks on all sides in hot oil; remove from pan. Set aside and keep warm.

Add onions, mushrooms, turnips and celery to drippings in pan; sauté until transparent and beginning to brown slightly. Add flour; stir to brown lightly. Stir in tomato paste, rosemary, thyme, bay leaf, garlic and stock. Return lamb shanks to pan. Bring mixture to a boil.

Cover and bake in a preheated 350-degree oven 2 hours, or until tender. Remove lamb shanks to a hot serving platter; keep warm. Skim fat from mixture in pan; spoon mixture over lamb shanks and serve hot.

MADD needs your continued support to end drunk driving.

Chicken Liver Risotto

Beth W. Orenstein
Staff Writer, *The Express-Times*, Easton, PA

This is my absolute favorite way to prepare chicken livers. The recipe calls for Swiss cheese, but when I don't have any on hand, I use other cheeses, such as Cheddar, which change the flavor slightly. I particularly like to serve this hearty dish on a winter evening. Everything, including the rice, cooks in one pot, which makes clean-up a snap.

Makes 4 to 5 servings

2 tablespoons butter or margarine
1 tablespoon vegetable oil
8 ounces chicken livers,
    trimmed and halved
2 tablespoons chopped onion
1 cup uncooked rice
2 cups chicken broth

1/2 teaspoon salt, or to taste
    (optional)
1 tablespoon spicy mustard
1 cup shredded Swiss cheese
2 tablespoons grated
    Parmesan cheese
Minced fresh parsley

Heat butter and oil in a medium skillet. Add halved chicken livers and chopped onion; cook 5 minutes, or until browned. Add rice; cook, stirring, 3 to 5 minutes, or until rice is lightly browned. Add broth. Simmer, covered, 20 to 25 minutes, or until liquid is absorbed and rice is tender. Taste and add salt, if needed. Stir in mustard and Swiss cheese. Sprinkle Parmesan cheese and parsley on top. Serve immediately.

Creole Hot Dogs

Jane Gray
Food Editor, *Ludington Daily News*, Ludington, MI

A friend, bemoaning the fact that her children wouldn't eat what they called "adult food," wanted a dish the whole family would enjoy. After some experimentation, she came up with this recipe, which she shared with me. The slight spiciness adds a Southern tang to "plain old hot dogs." Simple ingredients that are readily available make this a great supper choice on a busy night.

Makes 6 to 10 servings

5 slices bacon, diced
1/2 medium onion, chopped
1 cup unsweetened
    pineapple juice
1/2 cup ketchup
1/8 teaspoon chili powder

Hot pepper sauce, to taste
12 hot dogs
1/4 cup chopped green
    bell pepper
Hot cooked rice (optional)

In a large skillet, cook bacon until done but not crisp. Add onion; cook until tender but not brown. Add pineapple juice, ketchup, chili powder and hot pepper sauce; mix well.

Score hot dogs diagonally at 1-inch intervals; add to mixture in skillet. Cover; bring to a boil. Add bell pepper. Simmer, covered, 8 to 10 minutes. Serve over rice, if desired.

60% of pedestrians (16 yrs. and older) killed in nighttime crashes in 1991 had very high BACs (.10% or more).

Curried Rack of Lamb

Kasey Wilson
Food Columnist, *The Vancouver Courier*, Vancouver, BC, Canada

Lamb is often associated with festive events. This recipe for rack of lamb, seasoned with curry, garlic and ginger, captures the splendor of lamb, but it is so quick and easy it can be served any day of the week.

Makes 4 to 6 servings

2 racks of lamb (7 to 9 ribs each)	4 teaspoons curry powder
1 teaspoon salt	1 tablespoon grated lemon peel
3 cloves garlic, minced	1 tablespoon olive oil
2 teaspoons minced fresh ginger	1/4 teaspoon cayenne pepper

Have the butcher trim the fat from the lamb and "french the ribs to the eye." That means cutting down each rib bone halfway to the base and removing the strip of fat. Also, ask to have the rack cut through the lower bone so that you can carve the lamb easily between the ribs.

In a small bowl, combine salt, garlic and ginger to make a paste. Add curry powder, lemon peel, olive oil and cayenne; mix well.

Spread curry mixture evenly over top and sides of lamb racks. Place racks, fat-side up, in roasting pan. Insert meat thermometer into center of rack, making sure tip does not touch bone. Roast in a preheated 400-degree oven 45 minutes, or until the thermometer registers 140 degrees for rare, 160 degrees for medium or 170 degrees for well-done. Allow racks to stand 15 minutes before carving.

Curry in a Hurry

Mary D. Scourtes
Food Writer, *The Tampa Tribune*, Tampa, FL

This recipe is made-to-order for "planovers," the scraps of leftover lamb that we have after Sunday dinner. The recipe also works well with leftover chicken or pork.

Makes 6 servings

2 tablespoons olive oil
2 ribs celery, diced
2 small onions, chopped
1 apple, chopped
1 package (6 ounces) dried
   apricots, chopped

1/4 cup hot water
2 teaspoons curry powder
2 cups diced cooked lamb
1/4 cup heavy cream
Hot cooked rice

Heat olive oil in large skillet. Add celery, onions, apple, apricots and hot water; cook 5 to 6 minutes. Add curry powder and diced lamb. Bring to a boil; reduce heat. Simmer, covered, 10 to 12 minutes. Mix well. Add cream; heat 3 to 4 minutes. Serve over rice.

Ginger Chops

Jane Baker
Free-Lance Writer, East Lansing, MI

Lamb chops are great on the grill — an elegant treat for family or guests and so, so easy to prepare. I like lamb cooked rather rare, so I often use chops that are 1-1/4-inches thick. If you like lamb that is more well done, try using chops that are 3/4- to 1-inch thick. Serve chops with a wild rice pilaf or buttered egg noodles and a green vegetable or salad.

Makes 4 servings

1 tablespoon olive oil
1 teaspoon ground ginger
1/2 teaspoon garlic pepper
   (a seasoning blend)

4 lamb chops (1 1/4-inches thick)

Over half of all alcohol-related traffic fatalities occur in single-vehicle crashes.

In a small bowl, combine oil, ginger and garlic pepper; mix well. Brush mixture on both sides of lamb chops. Grill lamb chops over hot coals or under a preheated broiler about 5 minutes on each side, or until done to taste.

Greek-Style Lamb Kabobs

Susan Manlin Katzman
Free-Lance Food Writer, St. Louis, MO

In the late 1960s, my husband and I and our two children (ages 6 and 7) took a five-month camping trip through Europe. Although not picky eaters, the children were so-so about food and missed their familiar American fare — until we got to Greece and they had a taste of Souvlakia. It was love at first bite. Good-bye, hot dogs. So long, hamburgers. Souvlakia was the new sensation and they couldn't get enough of it. Good thing these lamb kabobs were as readily available at street stands in Greece as hot dogs are available in the States. After returning home, the kids begged for Souvlakia. It was always the dish they requested for special meals and the dish they most remember from their early introduction to European foods. I still serve it today, and the kids, who now have kids of their own, still love it. Incidentally, their kids like it, too.

Makes 12 to 14 servings

1 boneless leg of lamb (about 6 pounds)	About 3 1/2 tablespoons dried oregano, divided
1 cup olive oil	Salt, to taste
5 large lemons, divided	

Cut lamb into 1-inch cubes. Put cubes in a large glass bowl; gently stir in olive oil, juice of 4 lemons and 3 tablespoons oregano. Refrigerate, covered, several hours, stirring occasionally.

When ready to cook, drain lamb, discarding marinade. Thread lamb onto skewers. Broil or grill lamb 4 inches from heat source, turning occasionally, until browned on the outside but still pink inside. (The kabobs cook a total of about 11 minutes.)

Remove lamb from heat and place, skewers and all, on a serving plate. Sprinkle with remaining 1/2 tablespoon oregano, salt and the juice of the remaining 1 lemon. Serve immediately.

Lamb Chops with Orange-Apricot Couscous

Debra Carr-Elsing
Food Writer, *The Capital Times*, Madison, WI

This recipe makes use of couscous, the Middle Eastern specialty that is now readily available in the United States. Although I prefer this family recipe with lamb chops, it also can be prepared with pork chops. The combination of orange peel, apricots and spices gives this recipe a delicate flavor. It's a skillet dinner that doesn't take a lot of time to prepare at the end of a busy day.

Makes 4 servings

1 tablespoon vegetable oil
4 lamb chops
   ($1/2$- to $3/4$-inch thick)
$3/4$ cup chopped red or green
   bell pepper
$1/2$ cup sliced green onions
   (green and white parts)
1 $1/2$ cups orange juice

1 cup uncooked couscous
$1/2$ cup chopped dried apricots
1 teaspoon grated orange peel
$1/2$ teaspoon salt
$1/4$ teaspoon ground allspice
$1/4$ teaspoon ground ginger
$1/8$ teaspoon freshly ground
   black pepper

Heat oil in a large skillet over medium heat. Add lamb chops; cook about 4 minutes on each side, or until browned and cooked to taste. Remove chops from skillet and reserve.

Drain skillet, reserving 1 tablespoon drippings in the skillet. Add bell pepper and green onions to skillet; cook, stirring, until tender-crisp. Add orange juice, couscous, apricots, orange peel, salt, allspice, ginger and pepper; mix well. Put lamb chops over mixture in skillet. Bring mixture to a boil. Reduce heat to low. Simmer, covered, 3 to 5 minutes, or until liquid is absorbed and couscous is cooked. Fluff couscous lightly with a fork before serving.

About 57% of all traffic fatalities were alcohol-related on July 4th in 1991.

Lamb Shanks with Potatoes and Blue Cheese

Teri M. Grimes
Assistant Features Editor, *The Bradenton Herald*, Bradenton, FL

I will admit I'm nutty about blue cheese. Having perfected the ultimate quiche using this pungent cheese, I turned my sights in a different direction: lamb. At times, lamb is an incredible bargain, especially if you buy the cuts no one else seems interested in buying — namely the shoulder or shank. The great thing about this recipe is its ease of preparation. It's a one-dish meal with gourmet taste. Serve it for company — it's sure to get raves!

Makes 4 servings

1/4 cup olive oil
4 pounds lamb shanks or shoulder
   steaks (if using shanks, slice
   through to the bone)
2 pounds small potatoes, peeled
   and cut in half lengthwise
1 pound small white onions
1 can (16 ounces) tomatoes,
   undrained
1 can (6 ounces) tomato paste

1 clove garlic, minced
   (or more, to taste)
3/4 cup water
2 tablespoons red wine vinegar
2 teaspoons salt
3 small bay leaves
1 (3-inch) strip lemon peel
1/2 cup blanched slivered
   almonds
1/4 pound blue cheese, crumbled

Heat oil in a heavy Dutch oven. Add lamb shanks; brown on all sides. Remove meat from pan and set aside.

Add potatoes and onions to drippings in pan; cook until brown. Return lamb shanks to pan.

In container of an electric blender, combine tomatoes with their liquid, tomato paste, garlic, water, vinegar and salt. Blend until smooth. Pour tomato mixture over lamb shanks. Add bay leaves and lemon peel. Simmer, covered, 1 1/2 hours, or until lamb is tender.

Sprinkle almonds and blue cheese over lamb. Serve immediately.

Medallions of Venison with Blueberries

Kasey Wilson
Food Columnist, *The Vancouver Courier*, Vancouver, BC, Canada

If you don't have a hunter in your family, you can still enjoy venison by purchasing farm-raised venison — lean, tender and mild-tasting red meat from domesticated deer raised in New Zealand and in some states in the United States. Cooking venison loin in butter is a simple preparation method with delicious results. I like to serve venison rare or medium-rare.

Makes 4 servings

8 tablespoons unsalted
    butter, divided
4 venison medallions, cut from
    the loin (about 5 ounces each)
2 tablespoons finely
    chopped shallots

1/2 cup apple juice
1 cup chicken broth
Salt and freshly ground black
    pepper, to taste
1 cup fresh or frozen blueberries

Heat 2 tablespoons butter in a large skillet. Add venison; sauté, turning venison to brown both sides; cook until rare or done to taste. Transfer to a platter and keep warm.

Add shallots to the pan drippings in the skillet; sauté until soft. Deglaze pan with apple juice and broth; cook over high heat to reduce mixture to 1/2 cup. Lower heat to medium and whisk in remaining 6 tablespoons butter, 1 tablespoon at a time. Add blueberries; heat through.

Place 1 venison medallion on each serving plate; spoon one-fourth of the blueberry sauce over each serving.

More than 52% of all traffic deaths during the Thanksgiving weekend were alcohol-related in 1991.

Moussaka with Zucchini or Eggplant

Clara H. Eschmann
Food Columnist, *The Macon Telegraph*, Macon, GA

> *After a trip to Greece, I wanted to try my hand at Moussaka, which was one of my favorite foods in Greece. I tried several recipes, but none seemed right. So, I called a Greek friend who lives in Macon. She gave me her grandmother's recipe, which is delicious and easy to prepare.*

Makes 4 to 6 servings

2 tablespoons olive oil
3 small zucchini, unpeeled and
    cut into 1/4-inch slices
    (or 1 medium eggplant,
    unpeeled and cut into
    1/4-inch slices)
1 large onion, sliced
1 pound lean ground lamb

1 can (8 ounces) tomato sauce
1 clove garlic, minced
3/4 teaspoon salt
1/2 teaspoon ground cinnamon
1 cup diced feta cheese
1/4 to 1/2 cup grated
    Parmesan cheese

Heat oil in a large skillet. Add zucchini (or eggplant) and onion; cook until tender-crisp. Remove zucchini mixture from skillet and put in a 2-quart baking dish; set aside.

In the same skillet, brown lamb, stirring with a spoon to break up meat. Drain off fat. In a small bowl, combine tomato sauce, garlic, salt and cinnamon; pour over lamb; mix well. Simmer 10 to 15 minutes.

Spread lamb mixture evenly over zucchini mixture in baking dish. Sprinkle feta cheese and Parmesan cheese over top, covering completely. Bake in a preheated 350-degree oven 30 minutes. Serve hot.

About 47% of all traffic fatalities during Christmas were alcohol-related in 1991.

Oriental Liver

Teri M. Grimes
Assistant Features Editor, *The Bradenton Herald*, Bradenton, FL

When I was a child, Sunday dinner invariably meant liver — and that was my cue to ask my best friend if I could come to her house for dinner. When my mother espoused the benefits of eating liver, her words fell on deaf ears. But she was relentless in her pursuit of a liver recipe I would eat. She finally met with success with this recipe for Oriental Liver. Serve it over rice or Chinese noodles and watch liver-haters suddenly find a reason to stay home for dinner.

Makes 4 to 6 servings

1/4 cup all-purpose flour
1 1/2 teaspoons salt
1/4 teaspoon black pepper
1 1/2 pounds beef liver
2 tablespoons vegetable oil
2 medium onions, thinly sliced
1 green bell pepper, cut
    lengthwise into strips

1 tomato, cut into wedges
1 tablespoon grated fresh ginger
1 1/2 cups beef broth
Hot cooked rice or
    Chinese noodles

In a shallow bowl or on a sheet of waxed paper, combine flour, salt and pepper. Cut liver into serving-size pieces. Dredge liver in flour mixture.

Heat oil in a large skillet. Add liver; sauté 4 minutes on each side, or until cooked to taste. Do not overcook. Remove liver from skillet and reserve.

Add onions and bell pepper to skillet. Sauté until tender-crisp, adding more oil, if needed. Stir in tomato and ginger; sauté 2 minutes. Remove vegetables from skillet and reserve.

Add beef broth to skillet; bring to a boil, stirring and scraping pan. Return liver and vegetables to skillet; heat through. Serve over rice or Chinese noodles.

Roasted Leg of Lamb

Jane Baker
Free-Lance Writer, East Lansing, MI

There is nothing so elegant or so easy to prepare as a roasted leg of lamb. I often serve this recipe to guests because lamb is something different from the usual guest fare. It's easy on the cook, because once you put it in the oven, the lamb needs no other attention until it's carved and served. Although I have prepared lamb with many different seasonings, my favorite is a combination of rosemary and garlic pepper. To complete the meal, add steamed red potatoes and a salad made with butter lettuce, mandarin oranges and poppy seed dressing.

Makes 6 to 8 servings

1 leg of lamb (5 to 6 pounds)
1 to 2 tablespoons olive oil
1 tablespoon dried rosemary
2 teaspoons garlic pepper
    (a seasoning blend)

1 teaspoon coarsely ground
    black pepper (optional)
1/3 cup water or chicken broth
    (optional)

Put lamb on a rack in a shallow roasting pan. Brush oil over lamb. Sprinkle with rosemary, garlic pepper and, if desired, black pepper. Lightly rub seasonings into lamb. Bake in a preheated 325-degree oven 25 to 30 minutes per pound, or to an internal temperature of 175 degrees for medium-rare. Do not cover or baste lamb while it is cooking. Allow roast to stand 10 to 15 minutes, then carve and serve.

If desired, deglaze the roasting pan. Add about 1/3 cup water or chicken broth to drippings in pan. Cook on top of the stove, scraping drippings from the bottom of the pan. Serve glaze over sliced lamb.

Ruby Lamb

Narcisse S. Cadgène
Free-Lance Writer, New York, NY

This scrumptious stir-fry dish is lovely to behold because the sauce is such a brilliant red. Lamb takes well to stir-frying, and even tough cuts turn out fork-tender, if they are not overcooked. Resist the temptation to add more sauce to the lamb before cooking, and don't be worried that the recipe doesn't seem to make much sauce — it's a small quantity, but it packs a wallop.

Makes 4 servings

1 small red bell pepper, chopped
1/4 cup white vinegar
3 tablespoons granulated sugar
1/4 teaspoon crushed red pepper

3/4 teaspoon salt, divided
1 1/2 to 2 pounds lean
    boneless lamb
2 tablespoons vegetable oil

In container of an electric blender, combine bell pepper, vinegar, sugar, crushed red pepper and 1/4 teaspoon salt. Purée until well blended. Pour mixture into a small saucepan; bring to a boil. As soon as the mixture begins to thicken slightly (after about 1 minute), remove from heat. Set sauce aside.

Trim any fat or sinew from lamb; slice it into strips no more than 1/4-inch thick and 1-inch wide. (Partly freezing the meat makes slicing easier.) Toss lamb strips with 2 tablespoons of the sauce.

In a wok or large skillet, heat oil until quite hot. Add lamb; stir-fry until the lamb is hot through and pink juices begin to seep out. Do not overcook. Season lamb with remaining 1/2 teaspoon salt. Turn out onto heated serving platter or 4 serving plates. Place 1 tablespoon sauce on each plate; pass remaining sauce at the table.

Please don't drink and drive.

Spicy Lamb and Lentil Stew

Lori Longbotham
Free-Lance Food Writer, Astoria, NY

This stew has a warm, sunny flavor that is both homey and exotic. It's a good idea to toss the ingredients together and let the stew cook while you're preparing tonight's dinner, then reheat the stew tomorrow and serve it with almost no effort. Add rice pilaf and a green salad for a full meal.

Makes 8 servings

Water
2 cups dried lentils, rinsed
    and picked over
6 tablespoons olive oil, divided
2 pounds boneless lean
    lamb shoulder or neck,
    cut into 1-inch cubes
2 medium onions, diced
2 tablespoons paprika
2 tablespoons minced garlic
2 teaspoons freshly
    ground nutmeg

2 cans (16 ounces each)
    Italian tomatoes,
    drained and chopped
4 cups beef broth
Salt and cayenne pepper, to taste
1/4 cup fresh lemon juice
48 brine-cured olives, pitted
2 tablespoons minced fresh
    mint or parsley

Bring 2 1/2 quarts cold water to boiling in a large stockpot. Add lentils; boil 10 minutes. Drain lentils; set aside to cool.

Meanwhile, heat 3 tablespoons olive oil in a large Dutch oven over medium-high heat. Add half of the lamb cubes; cook 5 minutes, or until evenly browned on all sides, stirring frequently. Remove lamb and reserve. Repeat with remaining 3 tablespoons olive oil and remaining lamb cubes; remove lamb and reserve.

Add onions to Dutch oven; cook 5 minutes. Return reserved lamb to pan. Stir in paprika, garlic and nutmeg. Cook, stirring, 2 minutes. Add tomatoes and beef broth. Season with salt and cayenne. Bring to a boil. Reduce heat to medium-low. Simmer, covered, about 1 1/2 hours, or until lamb is almost tender, stirring occasionally.

Add drained lentils and more broth or some water, if necessary. Simmer, uncovered, 20 minutes, or until lamb and lentils are done. Stir in lemon juice just before serving. Taste and adjust seasonings. Top with olives and mint. Serve hot.

Remember that all forms of alcoholic beverages are drugs.

Veal with Chanterelles

Kasey Wilson
Food Columnist, *The Vancouver Courier*, Vancouver, BC, Canada

Chanterelles are orange-yellow, trumpet-shaped members of the mushroom family. You will find fresh ones in the market in the fall. They have a delicate apricot aroma. Do not overcook them, because they will become tough. Other mushrooms can be substituted if chanterelles are not in season.

Makes 4 servings

6 tablespoons clarified butter, divided
1 tablespoon minced garlic
1 tablespoon minced green onions
Salt and freshly ground black pepper

1/2 pound fresh chanterelles, rinsed, drained and sliced
1 1/3 pounds veal scallops
All-purpose flour, for dredging
2 eggs, beaten
1 tablespoon minced fresh parsley

Heat 3 tablespoons butter in a heavy skillet. Add garlic and green onions; cook briefly over medium heat. Sprinkle salt and pepper on sliced chanterelles; add to garlic mixture. Cook over medium heat, stirring occasionally.

Season veal with salt and pepper. Dredge lightly in flour; dip in beaten eggs. In a separate skillet, heat remaining 3 tablespoons butter. Add veal and cook 2 minutes; turn veal and cook 1 minute, or until done to taste.

Place veal on a serving platter. Spoon chanterelle mixture on top and sprinkle fresh parsley over all.

"Impaired" means a person's ability to drive safely is diminished by alcohol.

Venison Pepper Steak

Arlette Camp Copeland
Food Writer, *The Macon Telegraph*, Macon, GA

My husband is an avid deer hunter, and our family enjoys eating the meat he brings home every fall and winter. Originally, I prepared venison in the traditional country-style way, frying it with onions, garlic and mushrooms. When I became a food writer and more nutrition-conscious, I decided to find ways to lighten up the traditional recipes. Everyone in the family likes this recipe I developed. I usually serve it over rice, along with garlic bread and a green salad.

Makes 4 to 6 servings

1 1/2 pounds boneless venison,
   cut into strips
Black pepper
Garlic powder
1 to 2 tablespoons vegetable oil
2 medium onions, sliced
1/2 pound fresh
   mushrooms, sliced
1 to 2 green or red bell peppers,
   cut into 1-inch cubes

1/2 pound broccoli florets
3 tablespoons soy sauce
1 cup beef broth
2 tablespoons cornstarch
1/4 cup water
2 tomatoes, cut into wedges
3 to 4 cups hot cooked rice

Liberally season venison with pepper and garlic powder. Heat oil in a wok or large heavy non-stick skillet. Add venison; cook until brown. Add onions, mushrooms, bell peppers, broccoli and soy sauce; mix well. Stir-fry 5 minutes. Add beef broth; heat through. Mix cornstarch and water until smooth; add to mixture in wok. Cook, stirring, until sauce thickens. Add tomatoes; cook 3 to 4 minutes. Do not let tomatoes become mushy. Serve over rice.

Note: If you like spicy food, add cayenne pepper, to taste.

Venison Roast, German Style

Barbara Gibbs Ostmann
Food Writer, St. Louis, MO

My sister used to sample my husband's wild game entrées with a hint of suspicion but an adventurous spirit. Then she became engaged to a hunter — and suddenly she was interested in all of our game recipes. This one has become as big a favorite with them as it is with us. A German couple shared this recipe with me years ago, and I have used it ever since. With today's concern for fat and cholesterol, some people might balk at the bacon, butter and cream — but you don't eat this dish that often! The preparation is simple, and once you put the roast in the oven, you don't have to worry about it until time to make the gravy.

Makes 4 to 8 servings

1 venison roast (4 to 5 pounds)	1/2 cup dairy sour cream
3/4 cup butter or margarine	1/2 cup all-purpose flour
Salt and black pepper, to taste	1/2 cup half-and-half or
6 slices bacon	light cream
1 cup hot water	

Carefully trim any fat from venison. Melt butter in skillet. Add venison and lightly brown on all sides. Season generously with salt and pepper. Transfer meat and melted butter to roasting pan (a clay cooker works well). Place bacon slices over the top of the roast. Deglaze skillet with 1 cup hot water, scraping up any bits from bottom of skillet; pour over venison. Cover and bake in a preheated 350-degree oven 2 to 2 1/2 hours, or until done to taste. Baste with pan juices several times during cooking. About 30 minutes before roast is done, remove roast from oven to make gravy.

Combine sour cream, flour and half-and-half; stir until smooth. Pour mixture into juices in roasting pan; stir well. (It may be necessary to remove meat in order to stir mixture into juices; return meat to pan.)

Return pan to oven. Reduce oven temperature to 325 degrees. Continue baking for last 30 minutes of cooking time, basting venison occasionally with gravy.

Slice the roast and serve it with the gravy. To complete the German-style meal, serve boiled potatoes, cooked red cabbage and cranberry relish.

A person's ability to drive is impaired at blood alcohol content levels as low as .02.

Venison Salad

Arlette Camp Copeland
Food Writer, *The Macon Telegraph*, Macon, GA

As parents of three children, my husband and I seldom dine at home alone. One night this summer, however, all the children were eating away from home with friends. After working all day, I wanted something good but quick. This Venison Salad is what I prepared, using the fresh vegetables I had on hand. I served it with iced tea and toasted French bread topped with garlic butter.

Makes 2 to 4 servings

1 pound boneless venison,
   cut into strips
Black pepper
Garlic powder
2 to 3 tablespoons vegetable oil
1 leek, chopped
2 tablespoons Worcestershire
   sauce
2 tablespoons soy sauce
2 tablespoons balsamic vinegar
Fresh spinach, rinsed, drained
   and chopped

1 cup chopped tomato
6 to 8 green onions, chopped
   (green and white parts)
1/2 cup pitted black olives
1/2 cup cubed Swiss cheese
1/2 cup freshly grated
   Parmesan cheese
Additional balsamic vinegar and
   cayenne pepper, to taste
   (optional)

Season venison with pepper and garlic powder. Heat oil in a wok or large skillet. Add venison, leek, Worcestershire sauce, soy sauce and balsamic vinegar. Stir-fry until venison is medium done; do not overcook, or meat will toughen. Turn off heat and let venison sit in sauce while you prepare serving plates.

Put a generous portion of spinach on each plate. Drain venison, reserving sauce; spoon venison over spinach. Top with tomatoes, green onions, olives, Swiss cheese and Parmesan cheese. Spoon reserved sauce over each salad. If desired, season each serving with additional balsamic vinegar and a dash of cayenne.

Index

A

Alfalfa Sprouts
Glorified Steamed Veggies with Rice, 21

Almonds
Lamb Shanks with
    Potatoes and Blue Cheese, 143
Shrimp Casserole, 51

Apples
Knockwurst and Cabbage, 93
Medallions of Venison with
    Blueberries, 144
Simple Sauté, 102
Southern Pork Jumble, 105
Tuna Medallions with Sesame Seeds, 58

Apricots
Curry in a Hurry, 140
Elegantly Easy Chicken, 71
Fruit-Glazed Ham, 92
Lamb Chops with
    Orange-Apricot Couscous, 142

Artichokes
Greek Spaghetti, 22

Avocado
Vegetarian Taco Salad, 35

B

Bacon
Creole Hot Dogs, 138
Hamburger and Beans, 124
Jalapeño Chicken Curls, 76
Quick Cassoulet, 99
Venison Roast, German Style, 152

Bamboo Shoots
Mongolian Beef, 127
Moo-Goo-Gai-Pan Fajitas, 78

Beans
Aztec Chili, 62
Quick Cassoulet, 99

Spicy Rice and Beans, 32
Taco Casserole, 134
Vegetarian Taco Salad, 35

Beef
Beef and Eggplant Casserole, 110
Beef Macaroni Skillet, 111
Beef Stroganoff, 112
Beefed-Up Kabobs, 113
Cabbage Unrolled, 114
Campfire Stew, 115
Different Hamburgers, 116
East Meets West Pepper Steak, 117
Fabulous Fajitas, 118
Filet of Beef with Herb Butter, 119
Firehouse Meatballs, 120
Great Flank Steak, 121
Green Chili Stew, 122
Grilled Beef with Mustard Sauce, 123
Hamburger and Beans, 124
Hamburgers à la Venezia, 125
Hungarian Beef Pot, 125
Lean Picadillo, 126
Mongolian Beef, 127
Ogeechee River Goulash, 128
Seven League Pizzaburger, 129
Spaghetti Nest Pie, 130
Spanish Steak, 131
Spicy Grilled Steak, 132
Steak au Roquefort, 133
Taco Casserole, 134

Bell Peppers
Beef and Eggplant Casserole, 110
Chicken Madrid, 67
Chicken with Hoisin Sauce, 68
Creole Hot Dogs, 138
East Meets West Pepper Steak, 117
Grilled Mussels with Curry Butter, 44
Lamb Chops with
    Orange-Apricot Couscous, 142
Mediterranean Stir-Fry, 26
Mushroom Casserole, 27
Ogeechee River Goulash, 128

Oriental Liver, 146
Pasta Provençale, 30
Pork Chops and Sweet Potatoes, 96
Ruby Lamb, 148
Sausage and Peppers, 100
Sausage-Stuffed Zucchini, 101
Seven League Pizzaburger, 129
Southern Pork Jumble, 105
Spanish Steak, 131
Tuna Steaks Provençale, 59
Turkey Black Bean Chili, 85
Turkey Sausage Italiano, 87
Venison Pepper Steak, 151

Black Beans
Black Bean Salad Española, 19
Turkey Black Bean Chili, 85

Blueberries
Medallions of Venison with
    Blueberries, 144

Broccoli
Dieter's Stir-Fry, 42
Glorified Steamed Veggies with Rice, 21
Laotian Seafood Stir-Fry, 45
Mongolian Beef, 127
Venison Pepper Steak, 151

C

Cabbage
Cabbage Unrolled, 114
Corned Beef and Cabbage
    for the '90s, 116
Knockwurst and Cabbage, 93
Moo-Goo-Gai-Pan Fajitas, 78
Simple Sauté, 101

Capers
Lean Picadillo, 126

Carrots
Campfire Stew, 115
Glorified Steamed Veggies with Rice, 21
Knockwurst and Cabbage, 93
Laotian Seafood Stir-Fry, 46
Lentil-Vegetable Casserole, 24
Moo-Goo-Gai-Pan Fajitas, 78
Peasant Pork Chops, 95
Quick Cassoulet, 99
Savory Chicken Breasts, 83

Cashews
Chicken with Hoisin Sauce, 68
Elegantly Easy Chicken, 71
Tuna Casserole Deluxe, 57

Cauliflower
Glorified Steamed Veggies with Rice, 21
Laotian Seafood Stir-Fry, 46

Celery
Braised Lamb Shanks, 136
Curry in a Hurry, 140
Dieter's Stir-Fry, 42
East Meets West Pepper Steak, 117
Greenbrier Chicken Salad, 72
Ogeechee River Goulash, 128
Quick Cassoulet, 99
Shrimp Jambalaya, 52

Chanterelles
Veal with Chanterelles, 150

Cheese
Baked Deviled Eggs, 18
Baked Shrimp with Feta Cheese, 40
Beef and Eggplant Casserole, 110
Brie Strata with Fruit Salsa, 20
Chicken Breast Roasted with
    Spinach and Cheese, 65
Chicken Italiano, 66
Chicken Liver Risotto, 137
Easy Chicken Tetrazzini, 69
Glorified Steamed Veggies with Rice, 21
Greek Spaghetti, 22
Green Spaghetti, 23
Italian-Style Broiled Fish, 45
Lamb Shanks with
    Potatoes and Blue Cheese, 143
Lentil-Vegetable Casserole, 24
Macaroni and Cheese Supreme, 25
Moussaka with
    Zucchini or Eggplant, 145
Mushroom Casserole, 27
Pasta Primavera Pronto, 29
Scrambled Egg Bake, 31
Seven League Pizzaburger, 129
Spaghetti Nest Pie, 130
Spanish Tofu, 31
Steak au Roquefort, 133
Stuffed Zucchini, 33
Taco Casserole, 134
Tuna Casserole Deluxe, 57

Vegetarian Taco Salad, 35
Venison Salad, 153
White Chili, 88
Zucchini Pie, 36

Chicken
Chicken à l'Orange, 63
Chicken à la Mode, 64
Chicken Breast Roasted with
    Spinach and Cheese, 65
Chicken Italiano, 66
Chicken Madrid, 67
Chicken with Hoisin Sauce, 68
Easy Chicken Tetrazzini, 69
Easy Crispy Chicken, 70
Elegantly Easy Chicken, 71
Greenbrier Chicken Salad, 72
Hotshot Chicken, 74
Inside-Out Chicken, 75
Jalapeño Chicken Curls, 76
Moo-Goo-Gai-Pan Fajitas, 78
Provençale Chicken, 80
Raspberry Chicken, 81
Savory Chicken Breasts, 83
Shanghai Chicken, 84

Chilies
Green Chili Stew, 122
White Chili, 88

Clams
Spaghetti with Clam Sauce, 54

Corn
Aztec Chili, 62

Corned Beef
Corned Beef and Cabbage
    for the '90s, 116

Cornish Hens
Plum-Glazed Cornish Hens, 79
Roasted Cornish Hens, 82

Couscous
Lamb Chops with
    Orange-Apricot Couscous, 142

Crab
Laotian Seafood Stir-Fry, 46

E

Eggplant
Beef and Eggplant Casserole, 110
Mediterranean Stir-Fry, 26
Moussaka with
    Zucchini or Eggplant, 145

Eggs
Baked Deviled Eggs, 18
Black Bean Salad Española, 19
Blue Ribbon Ham Loaf, 90
Brie Strata with Fruit Salsa, 20
Moo-Goo-Gai-Pan Fajitas, 78
Mushroom Casserole, 27
Mushroom Lover's Tart, 28
Scrambled Egg Bake, 31
Spaghetti Nest Pie, 130
Tuna Medallions with Sesame Seeds, 58
Turkey Fried Rice, 86
Veal with Chanterelles, 150
Zucchini Pie, 36

F

Fish
Baked Fish Fillets, 38
Baked Fish Supreme, 39
Barbecued Fish Fillets, 41
Dieter's Stir-Fry, 42
Easy Baked Fish in Sauce, 43
Italian-Style Broiled Fish, 45
Pacific Rim Salmon, 48
Stuffed Orange Roughy, 55
Tuna Casserole Deluxe, 57
Tuna Medallions with Sesame Seeds, 58
Tuna Steaks Provençale, 59
Tuna Steaks with Tomatillo Salsa, 60

G

Ginger
Curried Rack of Lamb, 139
Ginger Chops, 140
Herbed Turkey Breast, 73

Grapes
Warm Pork and Fruit Salad, 108

Green Beans
Mock Stir-Fry, 77
Provençale Chicken, 80

H

Ham
Blue Ribbon Ham Loaf, 90
Fruit-Glazed Ham, 92
Sugar and Anise Baked Ham, 106

Hot Dogs
Creole Hot Dogs, 138

J

Jalapeño
Jalapeño Chicken Curls, 76
Turkey Black Bean Chili, 85
White Chili, 88

Jicama
Sweet-Sour Tofu Stir-Fry, 34

K

Kiwifruit
Warm Pork and Fruit Salad, 108

L

Lamb
Braised Lamb Shanks, 136
Curried Rack of Lamb, 139
Curry in a Hurry, 140
Ginger Chops, 140
Greek-Style Lamb Kabobs, 141
Lamb Chops with
    Orange-Apricot Couscous, 142
Lamb Shanks with
    Potatoes and Blue Cheese, 143
Moussaka with
    Zucchini or Eggplant, 145
Roasted Leg of Lamb, 147
Ruby Lamb, 148
Spicy Lamb and Lentil Stew, 149

Leeks
Venison Salad, 153

Lemons
Baked Fish Fillets, 38
Baked Fish Supreme, 39
Easy Baked Fish in Sauce, 43
Greek-Style Lamb Kabobs, 141
Spicy Grilled Steak, 132

Lentils
Lentil-Vegetable Casserole, 24
Spicy Lamb and Lentil Stew, 149

Liver
Chicken Liver Risotto, 137
Oriental Liver, 146

Lobster
Laotian Seafood Stir-Fry, 46

M

Macaroni
Beef Macaroni Skillet, 111
Macaroni and Cheese Supreme, 25
Tuna Casserole Deluxe, 57

Mushrooms
Beef Stroganoff, 112
Braised Lamb Shanks, 136
Easy Chicken Tetrazzini, 69
Mediterranean Stir-Fry, 26
Mock Stir-Fry, 77
Mushroom Casserole, 27
Mushroom Lover's Tart, 28
Scallops Alfredo, 50
Shrimp Stroganoff, 53
Spanish Steak, 131
Stuffed Zucchini, 33
Sweet-Sour Tofu Stir-Fry, 34
Tuna Casserole Deluxe, 57
Venison Pepper Steak, 151

Mussels
Grilled Mussels with Curry Butter, 44

O

Okra
Mock Stir-Fry, 77

Olives
Greek Spaghetti, 22
Lean Picadillo, 126

Provençale Chicken, 80
Spicy Lamb and Lentil Stew, 149
Tuna Casserole Deluxe, 57
Tuna Steaks Provençale, 59
Vegetarian Taco Salad, 35
Venison Salad, 153

Onions
Aztec Chili, 62
Baked Fish Fillets, 38
Baked Fish Supreme, 39
Baked Shrimp with Feta Cheese, 40
Beef and Eggplant Casserole, 110
Beef Macaroni Skillet, 111
Beef Stroganoff, 112
Black Bean Salad Española, 19
Cabbage Unrolled, 114
Caribbean Pork, 91
Chicken Madrid, 67
Curry in a Hurry, 140
Dieter's Stir-Fry, 42
East Meets West Pepper Steak, 117
Easy Baked Fish in Sauce, 43
Firehouse Meatballs, 120
Glorified Steamed Veggies with Rice, 21
Greek Spaghetti, 22
Green Chili Stew, 122
Grilled Beef with Mustard Sauce, 123
Hamburgers à la Venezia, 125
Herbed Turkey Breast, 73
Knockwurst and Cabbage, 93
Lamb Chops with
    Orange-Apricot Couscous, 142
Lamb Steaks with
    Potatoes and Blue Cheese, 143
Laotian Seafood Stir-Fry, 46
Lean Picadillo, 126
Lean Pork Loin with
    Onions and Raisins, 94
Lentil-Vegetable Casserole, 24
Mediterranean Stir-Fry, 26
Moo-Goo-Gai-Pan Fajitas, 78
Mushroom Casserole, 27
Mushroom Lover's Tart, 28
Ogeechee River Goulash, 128
Oriental Liver, 146
Pacific Rim Salmon, 48
Pasta Provençale, 30
Peasant Pork Chops, 95

Pork Chops, Alsatian Style, 97
Raspberry Chicken, 81
Sausage and Peppers, 100
Sausage-Stuffed Zucchini, 101
Seven League Pizzaburger, 129
Shrimp Jambalaya, 52
Southern Pork Jumble, 105
Spanish Tofu, 31
Sun Scallops, 56
Turkey Black Bean Chili, 85
Turkey Fried Rice, 86
Turkey Sausage Italiano, 87
Vegetarian Taco Salad, 35
Venison Pepper Steak, 151
Venison Salad, 153
Zucchini Pie, 36

Oranges
Chicken à l'Orange, 63
Easy Baked Fish in Sauce, 43
Lamb Chops with
    Orange-Apricot Couscous, 142

P

Peanut Butter
Pork with Spicy Peanut Sauce, 98

Pears
Brie Strata with Fruit Salsa, 20
Pork Chops, Alsatian Style, 97

Peas
Chicken with Hoisin Sauce, 68
Laotian Seafood Stir-Fry, 46
Sweet-Sour Tofu Stir-Fry, 34

Pecans
Southern Pork Jumble, 105

Pineapple
Creole Hot Dogs, 138
Fruit-Glazed Ham, 92
Pacific Rim Salmon, 48
Pork Chops and Sweet Potatoes, 96
Sweet-Sour Tofu Stir-Fry, 34

Pine Nuts
Lean Pork Loin with
    Onions and Raisins, 94

Pork
Blue Ribbon Ham Loaf, 90
Caribbean Pork, 91

Lean Pork Loin with
  Onions and Raisins, 94
Peasant Pork Chops, 95
Pork Chops and Sweet Potatoes, 96
Pork Chops, Alsatian Style, 97
Pork with Spicy Peanut Sauce, 98
Slightly Cajun Pork Chops, 103
Soda Pop Chops, 104
Southern Pork Jumble, 105
Thyme for Pork Chops, 107
Warm Pork with Fruit Salad, 108

Potatoes
Campfire Stew, 115
Knockwurst and Cabbage, 93
Lamb Shanks with
  Potatoes and Blue Cheese, 143
Peasant Pork Chops, 95

R

Raisins
Lean Pork Loin with
  Onions and Raisins, 94

Raspberries
Raspberry Chicken, 81

Rice
Cabbage Unrolled, 114
Chicken à l'Orange, 63
Chicken Liver Risotto, 137
Chicken with Hoisin Sauce, 68
Curry in a Hurry, 140
East Meets West Pepper Steak, 117
Easy Crispy Chicken, 70
Glorified Steamed Veggies with Rice, 21
Mock Stir-Fry, 77
Mongolian Beef, 127
Ogeechee River Goulash, 128
Oriental Liver, 146
Shanghai Chicken, 84
Shrimp Casserole, 51
Shrimp Jambalaya, 52
Shrimp Stroganoff, 53
Spanish Tofu, 31
Spicy Rice and Beans, 32
Turkey Fried Rice, 86
Venison Pepper Steak, 151

S

Salsa
Black Bean Salad Española, 19
Hotshot Chicken, 74
Taco Casserole, 134

Sauerkraut
Pork Chops, Alsatian Style, 97

Sausage
Knockwurst and Cabbage, 93
Quick Cassoulet, 99
Sausage and Peppers, 100
Sausage-Stuffed Zucchini, 101
Simple Sauté, 102
Turkey Sausage Italiano, 87

Scallops
Scallops Acadia, 49
Scallops Alfredo, 50
Sun Scallops, 56

Shallots
Filet of Beef with Herb Butter, 119
Medallions of Venison with
  Blueberries, 144
Tuna Steaks with Tomatillo Salsa, 60

Shrimp
Baked Shrimp with Feta Cheese, 40
Laotian Seafood Stir-Fry, 46
New Orleans-Style
  Barbecued Shrimp, 47
Shrimp Casserole, 51
Shrimp Jambalaya, 52
Shrimp Stroganoff, 53

Spaghetti
Easy Chicken Tetrazzini, 69
Greek Spaghetti, 22
Pasta Primavera Pronto, 29
Spaghetti Nest Pie, 130
Spaghetti with Clam Sauce, 54
Spicy Grilled Steak, 132

Spinach
Campfire Stew, 115
Chicken Breast Roasted with
  Spinach and Cheese, 65
Venison Salad, 153

Squash
Pasta Provençale, 30

Strawberries
Brie Strata with Fruit Salsa, 20

Sweet Potatoes
Pork Chops and Sweet Potatoes, 96
Southern Pork Jumble, 105

T

Tofu
Spanish Tofu, 31
Sweet-Sour Tofu Stir-Fry, 34

Tomatoes
Aztec Chili, 62
Baked Shrimp with Feta Cheese, 40
Beef Macaroni Skillet, 111
Black Bean Salad Española, 19
Cabbage Unrolled, 114
Chicken à la Mode, 64
Chicken Madrid, 67
East Meets West Pepper Steak, 117
Green Chili Stew, 122
Italian-Style Broiled Fish, 45
Lamb Shanks with
    Potatoes and Blue Cheese, 143
Lentil-Vegetable Casserole, 24
Macaroni and Cheese Supreme, 25
Mediterranean Stir-Fry, 26
Mock Stir-Fry, 77
Moussaka with
    Zucchini or Eggplant, 145
Ogeechee River Goulash, 128
Oriental Liver, 146
Pasta Provençale, 30
Provençale Chicken, 80
Quick Cassoulet, 99
Sausage and Peppers, 100
Sausage-Stuffed Zucchini, 101
Shrimp Jambalaya, 52
Spaghetti Nest Pie, 130
Spanish Steak, 131
Spanish Tofu, 31
Spicy Lamb and Lentil Stew, 149
Spicy Rice and Beans, 32
Sun Scallops, 56
Tuna Steaks with Tomatillo Sauce, 60
Turkey Black Bean Chili, 85
Turkey Sausage Italiano, 87
Vegetarian Taco Salad, 35

Tortillas
Fabulous Fajitas, 118
Green Chili Stew, 122
Moo-Goo-Gai Pan Fajitas, 78
Taco Casserole, 134
Vegetarian Taco Salad, 35

Turkey
Aztec Chili, 62
Herbed Turkey Breast, 73
Mock Stir-Fry, 77
Turkey Black Bean Chili, 85
Turkey Fried Rice, 86
White Chili, 88

Turnips
Braised Lamb Shanks, 136

V

Veal
Veal with Chanterelles, 150

Venison
Medallions of Venison with
    Blueberries, 144
Venison Pepper Steak, 151
Venison Roast, German Style, 152
Venison Salad, 153

Y

Yogurt
Grilled Beef with Mustard Sauce, 123
Shrimp Stroganoff, 53
Taco Casserole, 134
Turkey Black Bean Chili, 85

Z

Zucchini
Glorified Steamed Veggies with Rice, 21
Moussaka with
    Zucchini or Eggplant, 145
Pasta Provençale, 30
Sausage-Stuffed Zucchini, 101
Stuffed Zucchini, 33
Sweet-Sour Tofu Stir-Fry, 34
Zucchini Pie, 36